... as a slave. I go through the world as a ... go back a human being. I ask to be deemed ... back with reputation and celebrity; for I am sure that if the Americans were to believe one tittle of all that has been said in this country respecting me, they would certainly admit me to be a little better than they had hitherto supposed I was. I return, but as a human being in better circumstances than when I came ...

His stay in Europe had strengthened Douglass' determination to ... what discrimination or, where and everywhere "I have made up my ... he announced. "wherever I go, I shall ... my ... ... When I go on board of your steamboat ... hall ... ... northern ... When ... ...

DOVER · THRIFT · EDITIONS

Frederick Douglass on Slavery and the Civil War

SELECTIONS FROM HIS WRITINGS

Edited and with an Introduction by
PHILIP S. FONER

DOVER PUBLICATIONS, INC.
Mineola, New York

DOVER THRIFT EDITIONS

GENERAL EDITOR: PAUL NEGRI
EDITOR OF THIS VOLUME: JOSLYN T. PINE

Bibliographical Note

Frederick Douglass on Slavery and the Civil War: Selections from His Writings, first published in 2003, is an unabridged republication of the work originally published in 1945 by International Publishers Co., Inc., New York.

Library of Congress Cataloging-in-Publication Data

Douglass, Frederick, 1818–1895.
    [Selections. 2003]
    Frederick Douglass on slavery and the Civil War : selections from his writings : edited and with an introduction by Philip S. Foner.
        p. cm. — (Dover thrift editions)
    Originally published as: Frederick Douglass. New York : International Publishers, 1945.
    ISBN 0-486-43171-1
    1. Antislavery movements—United States—History. 2. Slavery—United States—History. 3. United States—History—Civil War, 1861–1865—African Americans. 4. Reconstruction. I. Foner, Philip Sheldon, 1910– II. Title. III. Series.

E449.D737 2003
973.7—dc22

2003055600

Manufactured in the United States of America
Dover Publications, Inc., 31 East 2nd Street, Mineola, N.Y. 11501

Contents

A TRIBUNE OF HIS PEOPLE

by Philip S. Foner

NO GREATER dramatic proof of the contributions the Negro people have made to our democratic tradition can be offered than to cite the career of Frederick Douglass. From his early life until his death, on February 20, 1895, this great American, this great Negro, was concerned with the universal struggle for freedom of people everywhere. "Under the skin," he once observed, "we are all the same and every one of us must join in the fight to further human brotherhood." His biography is essentially the story of unceasing efforts "to further human brotherhood." Born a slave, he lifted himself up from bondage by his own efforts, taught himself to read and write, developed a great talent as a lecturer, editor, and organizer, became a noted figure in American life, and gained an international reputation as the spokesman for his people. An advocate of women's rights, labor solidarity, and full freedom for all regardless of race, creed, or color, Douglass represents the highest type of progressive leadership emerging from the ranks of the American people.

In its issue of June 28, 1879, the *Rochester Democrat and Chronicle* said of Douglass, whom it described as "among the greatest men, not only of this city, but of the nation as well—great in gifts, greater in utilizing them, great in his inspiration, greater in his efforts for humanity, great in the persuasion of his speech, greater in the purpose that informed it":

> "Frederick Douglass can hardly be said to have risen to greatness on account of the opportunities which the republic offers to self-made men, and concerning which we are apt to talk with an abundance of self-gratulation. To him, the republic offered no opportunities. It sought to fetter his mind equally with his body. For him, it builded no school-house, and for him it errected no church. So far as he was concerned, freedom was a mockery, and

1

law was the instrument of tyranny. In spite of law and gospel, despite of statutes which thralled him and opportunities which jeered at him, he made himself by trampling on the law and breaking through the thick darkness that encompassed him. There is no sadder commentary upon American slavery than the life of Frederick Douglass. He put it under his feet and stood erect in the majesty of his intellect; but how many intellects as brilliant and as powerful as his it stamped upon and crushed no mortal can tell until the secrets of its terrible despotism are fully revealed. Thanks to the conquering might of American freemen, such sad beginnings of such illustrious lives as that of Frederick Douglass are no longer possible; and that they are no longer possible is largely due to him who, when his lips were unlicked, became a deliverer of his people. Not alone did his voice proclaim emancipation. Eloquent as was that voice, his life, in its pathos and in its grandeur, was more eloquent still: and where shall be found, in the annals of humanity, a sweeter rendering of poetic justice than that he, who has passed through such vicissitudes of degradation and of exaltations, has been permitted to behold the redemption of his race?"

Douglass has told us the story of the early period of his life as a slave in his fascinating autobiographies.* The story merits retelling. He was born in Talbot County, Eastern Shore, Maryland, in the month of February (the exact year is unknown though it is commonly believed to be 1817). His father he never knew, and his mother he saw but seldom. Since she worked as a slave on a plantation twelve miles removed from her six children, he was cared for by his grandmother until he was five or six years of age. Once he was visited unexpectedly by his mother who had walked the twelve miles to see him and bring him a large gingercake. "I dropped off to sleep and waked in the morning to find my mother gone," he recalled years later. "I do not remember ever seeing her again. Death soon ended the little communication that had existed between us, and with it, I believe, a life full of weariness and heartfelt sorrow."

At the age of seven the lad was taken from his birthplace to the residence of his master, Captain Aaron Anthony, who served as manager of the vast plantations of Colonel Edward Lloyd. Here he discovered additional realities of slave life. For three years he was "so pinched with

---

*Douglass wrote three separate autobiographical studies, *Narrative of the Life of Frederick Douglass*, Boston, 1845; *My Bondage and My Freedom*, New York, 1855, and *Life and Times of Frederick Douglass*, Hartford, Conn., 1881. The last-mentioned volume represents the synthesis of his life's experience.

hunger as to dispute with old 'Nep,' the dog, for the crumbs which fell from the kitchen table." Often he followed "with eager step, the waiting girl when she shook the table cloth, to get the crumbs and small bones flung out for the dogs and cats." Such treatment made the young boy fully aware, even at the age of nine, of the "unjust and murderous character of slavery."

When ten years old, Douglass was sent by Captain Anthony to Baltimore to live with Hugh Auld, a relative of the Anthonys. For seven years he served Hugh Auld, first as a household servant and later as an unskilled laborer in his shipyard. Eager to learn to read and write, he begged his mistress to teach him. In response to his pleas, Mrs. Auld began to teach him to read, and before long young Douglass had mastered the alphabet "and could spell words of three or four letters." But the lessons ended the moment Mrs. Auld proudly told her husband of the boy's rapid progress. In Douglass' presence, Hugh Auld prohibited any further instruction on the ground that "learning would spoil any nigger." The words only served to increase the youth's determination to learn: "Very well, thought I, 'knowledge unfits a child to be a slave' . . . and from that moment I understood the direct pathway from slavery to freedom."

By various ingenious devices Douglass continued his education. He converted into teachers white children whom he met on the streets by having them help him with his Webster spelling book which he kept in his pocket. The first fifty cents he earned shining shoes went for the purchase of a popular schoolbook, the *Columbian Orator.* He devoured its contents, and from the speeches of Sheridan obtained "a bold and powerful denunciation of oppression and a most brilliant vindication of the rights of man."

When Douglass was eleven years of age, he was sent to his master's shipyards to beat and spin oakum, keep fires under pitch boilers and turn grindstones. During slack periods he mastered the essentials of writing by imitating the letters on the ships. Using the streets as his schools, his playmates as teachers, and the fences as his copybooks and blackboards, he learned to write. Once in later life he wrote in response to a request for his autograph: "Though my penmanship is not fine it will do pretty well for one who learned to write on a board fence."[1]

During these early years of his life Douglass searched for answers to the questions: "Why am I a slave? Why are some people slaves, and others masters? Was there ever a time when this was not so? How did the relation commence?" Hearing the Abolitionists denounced by his master and his friends, he resolved to discover "who and what the Abolitionists were." He found the answer in the columns of the *Baltimore American,* which featured the story that a vast number of petitions had been submitted to Congress, praying for the abolition of the internal slave trade. From that day on "there was hope in those words."

Upon the death of Captain Anthony the sixteen-year-old lad became the slave of Thomas Auld, a cruel and tight-fisted master. Determined to crush young Douglass' spirit, Auld turned him over to Edward Covey, a professional "Negro-breaker." From January to August, 1834, Douglass was overworked, flogged daily, and almost starved to death. After six months of such brutality, the youth made up his mind to fight back and when the time came soundly thrashed the "Negro-breaker." Convinced that it was too risky to try to "break" Douglass, Covey adopted a new approach and began to ignore him. The young slave never forgot the incident:

> "I was a changed being after that fight. I was nothing before, I was a man now . . . with a renewed determination to be a free man. . . . I had reached the point at which I was not afraid to die. This spirit made me a freeman in fact, though I still remained a slave in form."

After his battle with the "Negro-breaker," Douglass worked for two years on the plantation of a nearby slave-owner, William Freedland. Conditions were a good deal better here; he had sufficient food and enough leisure to conduct a secret Sunday school for forty slaves. But kindness, food and a few leisure hours were not enough. Early in 1836 Douglass resolved to escape and, together with several associates, prepared to seize a large canoe, paddle down the Chesapeake, and follow the North star to freedom. The plot was discovered, and Douglass was jailed. About to be sold to slave traders, his master had him sent back to Baltimore. Here he worked in the shipyards, caulking vessels.

At a meeting of the East Baltimore Improvement Society he met Anna Murray, a free Negro woman, and this meeting increased his desire to be free, for he was determined to marry as a man, not the property of a master.

On September 2, 1838, after much preparation, Frederick Douglass escaped from slavery. From a free Negro seaman he borrowed a sailor's "protection," a paper entitling the owner, whose description was outlined, to move about.* Posing as a free Negro sailor, Douglass boarded a train from Baltimore to Philadelphia. Many times during this trip he

---

*Douglass did not divulge the method of his escape until November, 1881, when he published an article in the *Century Magazine*, entitled "My Escape from Slavery." To have told the story before the close of the Civil War would have endangered the lives of those who assisted him, and revealed to slave owners a method employed by fugitive slaves.

was certain that he was about to be discovered, but fortunately the conductor did not trouble to compare his features with those described in the "protection." On September 3, Douglass arrived in Philadelphia where, in his own words, he "lived more in one day than in a year of . . . slave life." The next day he landed in New York City.

He soon discovered why Abolitionists referred to the Empire City as "the prolongation of the South," where "ten thousands cords of interests are linked with the Southern Slaveholder."[2] Here a fugitive slave was no safer than in Baltimore, and, in the midst of the panic of 1837, there were few opportunities for a free Negro to earn a livelihood. A passing sailor, to whom Douglass revealed his plight, introduced him to David Ruggles, the efficient Negro secretary of the New York Vigilance Committee, organized to aid fugitive slaves.[3] Ruggles sheltered him for several days, during which time Anna Murray joined him. On September 15, they were married by a Presbyterian minister, and a few days later the couple were on their way to New Bedford, Massachusetts, where Ruggles believed Douglass' skill as a caulker would gain them a livelihood.

Assisted by Mr. and Mrs. Nathan Johnson, a prosperous Negro family, the Douglasses settled down to their new life.* Unable to pursue his trade of caulking because of the opposition of white workingmen, Douglass was forced to saw wood, shovel coal, dig cellars, cart rubbish, blow bellows in a brass foundry, and load and unload vessels at one dollar a day. The family's meager income was supplemented by Anna's earnings as a domestic servant.

The day-to-day task of eking out an existence for a growing family—two children, Rosetta and Lewis, were born within two years after the family arrived in New Bedford—did not afford Douglass many opportunities to continue his education. But he applied the same ingenuity that had stood him in good stead as a slave. "Hard work, night and day, over a furnace hot enough to keep metal running like water was more favorable to action than thought," he wrote later, "yet here I often nailed a newspaper to the post near my bellows and read while I was performing the up and down motion of the heavy beam by which the bellows were inflated and discharged."

Learning that Negroes could attend the white Methodist churches in New Bedford only if they agreed to sit in separate pews, he refused to

---

*Johnson bestowed the name Douglass on his new friend. He had been named Frederick Augustus Washington Bailey by his mother, but had gradually dropped the two middle names and changed the last to Johnson. When he came to New Bedford, it was decided to change the Johnson because of the great number of Negroes with that name. Having just finished reading Scott's *Lady of the Lake*, Johnson suggested the name Douglass.

accept this humiliating condition and joined a small sect of his own people, the Zion Methodists. Soon he became a local preacher and attracted attention by his ability as a speaker. "It was in the Methodist prayer-meetings," a close friend of his once recalled, "that he found that he could speak so that every one would listen to him, and that few, if any, could speak as he could."[4]

Like so many other Negroes who had escaped from slavery, Douglass could not really feel free as long as his people remained in bondage.* Shortly after his arrival in New Bedford, he subscribed to the *Liberator*, the great anti-slavery journal edited by William Lloyd Garrison, a few weeks after arriving in New Bedford. Soon he was attending the Abolitionist meetings conducted by the Negro people of the community. On August 9, 1841, at one such meeting, Douglass delivered the first of many speeches calling for the freedom of the slaves. Joining in the discussion following Garrison's speech, Douglass made a favorable impression upon the anti-slavery leader. A few weeks later, at a grand anti-slavery convention in Nantucket, Douglass again spoke, this time relating his experiences as a slave. He electrified the audience by his convincing narrative, and Garrison, the next speaker, used the speech as his text.

After the convention, John A. Collins, general agent of the Massachusetts Anti-Slavery Society, urged Douglass to become an active lecturer for the organization. Reluctant at first to accept, Douglass finally agreed, and decided to devote his entire time to the cause of abolition. Together with Abby Kelly, S. S. Foster, Parker Pillsbury, and Garrison himself, Douglass lectured throughout the state and wherever he toured crowds listened attentively to his story. At a convention of the Worcester North Division Society during October, 1841, the members adopted a resolution welcoming "into their midst, Frederick Douglass, a fugitive from slavery, and extend[ing] to him the right hand of fellowship, as a co-worker in the great cause of human redemption. . . ."[5]

It was no simple matter to be an Abolitionist agent at this time, when, in many communities, hoodlums were hired to attack anti-slavery speakers and disrupt their meetings. It was especially difficult for a Negro, for he was forced to face the most humiliating discrimination while traveling, and was the first person set upon by thugs who would attack a meeting crying, "Get the nigger"; "kill the damn nigger." Yet Douglass, like other great Negro spokesmen in the Abolitionist movement , met these attacks, continued to bring the message of freedom to the people, and at the same time conducted a consistent battle against

---

*He felt this personally as well, since his three sisters and his brother were still in bondage.

discrimination which he correctly regarded as the direct result of the enslavement of the Negro people.*

Douglass' initial tour for the Massachusetts Anti-Slavery Society was eminently successful. In his annual report to the Society, John A. Collins bestowed lavish praise upon the young orator who had traveled with him to "upwards of sixty towns and villages":

> "Though he has never been favored with the advantages of an education, his style of speaking is chaste, free and forcible—his enunciation clear and distinct—his manner deliberate and energetic, alike free from tameness and ranting vehemence. His descriptions of slavery are most graphic, and his arguments are so lucid, and occasionally so spiced with pleasantry, and sometimes with a little satire, that his addresses, though long, are seldom tedious, but are listened to with the most profound respect. He is capable of performing a vast amount of good for his oppressed race."[6]

The report not only impressed the Massachusetts Society, but the Connecticut and Rhode Island Societies also engaged his services as a lecturer. And in 1843 the New England Anti-Slavery Society selected him as one of the speakers to appear at one hundred anti-slavery conventions from New Hampshire to Indiana. During his trip to the West, Douglass participated in the National Convention of Colored Men. Here he became better acquainted with other Negroes active in the anti-slavery movement, particularly William Wells Brown and Henry Highland Garnet, who, like himself, were escaped slaves.

Life was far from pleasant for Douglass and his colleagues during the convention tour. Audiences were often unreceptive and sometime distinctly hostile. In Newcastle, Indiana, a mob attacked the speakers and Douglass narrowly escaped being killed. In a letter to the *Liberator* of October 13, 1843, William A. White described the ordeal:

> ". . . Frederick Douglass who, at the time, was safe among the friends, not seeing me, thought I was knocked down, and seizing a club, rushed into the crowd. His weapon was immediately snatched from him. . . . [He] fled for his life, and ten or more of the mob followed crying, 'Kill the nigger, kill the damn nigger. . . .' The leader of the mob soon overtook him, and knocked him down and struck him once with his club, and was raising it the second time to level a blow which must have been fatal had it fallen, but

---

*"We are then a persecuted people," Douglass wrote in 1850, "not because we are *colored*, but simply because this color has for a series of years been coupled in the public mind with the degradation of slavery and servitude." (*The North Star*, June 13, 1850.)

I, by dint of hard running, came up in time to throw myself upon him, and stop him in his murderous purpose. . . . Frederick was taken up, and though at first he seemed to have been severely injured, he soon recovered and was able to lecture the next day."

Despite such incidents, the Hundred Conventions was truly a "magnificent movement" and, in January, 1844, the Massachusetts Anti-Slavery Society sponsored a similar number of conventions within the state. Again Douglass went on tour, and again he moved audiences with his magnificent oratory.

In the early stages of his career as an anti-slavery lecturer, Douglass' speeches were in most part accounts of his life as a slave. But soon he tired of repeating the same story and began to do more than recite facts. A number of his fellow Abolitionists criticized him for changing his method of presentation, arguing that his good English and perfect bearing caused many people to doubt whether he had ever been a slave. So Douglass resolved to publish the facts about his life as a slave, naming his master and giving dates and places. Those who doubted could then check the veracity of his statements.

During the winter months of 1844–1845, Douglass worked on the manuscript of the *Narrative of the Life of Frederick Douglass.* Wendell Phillips and other anti-slavery leaders advised him against publishing the story, pointing out that efforts would then be made to recapture him. But Douglass persisted and, in May, 1845, the book, prefaced by letters from Garrison and Phillips, made its appearance. Priced at fifty cents, it ran through a large edition.

In order to escape possible recapture, Douglass decided to go abroad. With a purse of $250 raised by his anti-slavery friends in Boston, he sailed for England in August, 1845, on the British ship *Cambria,* in company with the Hutchinsons, a family of Abolitionist singers, and James Buffum, vice-president of the Massachusetts Anti-Slavery Society.* Buffum made every effort to obtain a cabin for his Negro friend but was unsuccessful and Douglass was forced to make the voyage in steerage. But every morning he met his friends on the promenade deck and together they distributed copies of his *Narrative.* Impressed by the presence of an author on his ship, the captain invited

---

*In a letter to Gerrit Smith, Buffum wrote: "I write to inform you, that our friend and co-labourer Frederick Douglass has concluded to visit Europe this season, to lay before the people of that country the claims of the Slave. . . . He will go out as a representative from the prison-house of bondage and not as the representative from any Sect or party. He will stand up before that people as one who has experienced the withering and blighting influence of Slavery upon his own Soul. His friends are confident that he will be of great service to the cause, in exciting a deeper hatred in the breasts of the English people of American Slavery, and thereby creating a warmer sympathy for our

Douglass to lecture to the passengers on the night before the vessel docked at Liverpool. The lecture was broken up, but not before Douglass had expressed his opinions on slavery and segregation.

For two years Douglass traveled in England, Scotland, and Ireland. These were happy months. There was a complete absence of color prejudice and everywhere he went he addressed large and sympathetic audiences. His main subject, Slavery and Abolition, he also delivered several lectures on temperance and for the repeal of the Act of Union which had abolished the independent Irish parliament. Just what it meant to him to be able to live and breathe without being constantly reminded of his color is vividly set forth in his letters from Europe to the *Liberator*. Writing from Belfast on January 1, 1846, Douglass exulted:

> "The warm and generous cooperation extended to me by the friends of my despised race—the prompt and liberal manner with which the press has rendered me its aid—the glorious enthusiasm with which thousands have flocked to hear the cruel wrongs of my down-trodden and long enslaved countrymen portrayed—the deep sympathy of the slave, and the strong abhorrence of the slave-holder, everywhere evinced—the cordiality with which members and ministers of various religious bodies, and of various shades of religious opinion, have embraced me and lent me their aid—the kind hospitality constantly proferred to me by persons of the highest rank in society—the spirit of freedom that seems to animate all with whom I come in contact—and the entire absence of everything that looked like prejudice against me, on account of the color of my skin—contrasting so strongly with my long and bitter experience in the United States, that I look with wonder and amazement on the transition."[7]

But in other letters to the *Liberator* Douglass described at length the conditions of the working class in England, Scotland, and Ireland, and evinced his opposition to the exploitation of the poor. To those who objected to his concern with reforms other than anti-slavery, he replied:

> ". . . Though I am more closely connected and identified with one class of outraged, oppressed and enslaved people, I cannot

---

cause. When they shall see before them a man so noble and eloquent as Frederick, and learn from his own lips, that he is only seven years out of bondage; that he has now the marks of the whip upon his back, which he will carry with him until the day of his death, that he has near and dear relatives that are now pining in bondage; they will realize to a considerable extent the horrors of the American Slave trade; the effect cannot be otherwise than good. . . ." (James Buffum to Gerrit Smith, June 21, 1845, Gerrit Smith Papers, Syracuse University Library.)

allow myself to be insensible to the wrongs and suffering of any part of the great family of man. I am not only an American slave, but a man, and as such, am bound to use my powers for the welfare of the whole human brotherhood. . . . I believe that the sooner the wrongs of the whole human family are made known, the sooner those wrongs will be reached."[8]

In December, 1846, Frederick Douglass legally became a free person. Several English friends, especially Ellen and Anna Richardson of Newcastle, raised $750 and purchased his emancipation, placing the bill of sale in Douglass' hands.

Some Abolitionists in the United States were shocked at the news and were furious at Douglass for consenting to the purchase of his freedom, contending that it was a "violation of anti-slavery principles, conceding the right of property in man, and a wasteful expenditure of money." Douglass reminded them that it was a step of the utmost importance, for he would have been seized by his master and returned to slavery the moment he set foot in the United States.* He could have remained in England; indeed, his English friends were only too eager to assist him in establishing himself in the British Isles. But he refused. "I could have lived there," he informed the Anti-Slavery Convention in Boston upon his return to the United States, "but when I remembered this prejudice against color, as it is called, and slavery, and saw the many wrongs inflicted on my people at the North that ought to be combated and put down, I felt a disposition to lay aside ease, to turn my back on the kind offer of my friends, and to return among you—deeming it more noble to suffer along with my colored brethren, and meet these prejudices, than to live at ease, undisturbed, on the other side of the Atlantic."[9]

On his return voyage to America Douglass again met "Jim Crow." At Liverpool he was informed that he could not board the ship unless he agreed to travel in steerage, take his meals alone, and stay away from the saloon. He was forced to yield but, in a letter to the *London Times*, he described the incident, "sincerely believing that the British public will pronounce a just verdict on such proceedings."[10] It did! Popular indignation was so thoroughly aroused in England that the founder of the Cunard line was compelled publicly to give assurances that never again would such a shameful incident take place on his ships.

When Douglass left America in 1845 he was known only to audiences in this country. He returned two years later an international figure, a man who was looked upon in Europe as a living symbol of what

---

*After the passage of the Fugitive Slave Act of 1850, Douglass would not have been safe from seizure.

millions of Negro people in the United States could contribute to civilization once their chains of bondage were broken. Douglass told a British audience in his farewell speech,

". . . I go back to the United States, not as I landed here—I came as a slave; I go back as a free man. I came here a thing—I go back a human being. I came here despised and maligned—I go back with reputation and celebrity; for I am sure that if the Americans were to believe one tithe of all that has been said in this country respecting me, they would certainly admit me to be a little better than they had hitherto supposed I was. I return, but as a human being in better circumstances than when I came."[11]

His stay in Europe had strengthened Douglass' determination to combat discrimination anywhere and everywhere. "I have made up my mind," he announced, "wherever I go, I shall go as a man, and not as a slave. When I go on board of your steamboats, I shall always aim to be courteous and mild in deportment towards all with whom I come in contact, at the same time firmly and constantly endeavoring to assert my equal right as a man and a brother."[12]

Along with his other work as an anti-slavery agent, Douglass began preparations for the publication of an anti-slavery paper. Several journals, edited by Negroes, had already appeared in this country and, in 1843, Douglass himself had aided in the publication of *The Ram's Horn*, a newspaper which aimed to express the sentiments of the Negro population of New York State.[13] But most of these journals had gone out of circulation after a brief existence. Douglass hoped to establish a paper which by appearing regularly would constantly be "a powerful evidence that the Negro was too much of a man to be held a chattel."

Although $2,000 had been raised by friends in England to enable Douglass to launch his paper, Phillips, Garrison, and other Abolitionists in Boston opposed this plan on the ground that he did not have sufficient funds to ensure success and that he "would be far more serviceable as a public speaker than . . . as an editor."[14] So Douglass temporarily abandoned the project and devoted all of his energies to lecturing. But in September, 1847, in spite of Garrison's opposition, he decided to go ahead with his plans to publish his weekly.

On December 3, 1847, *The North Star*, with Frederick Douglass as editor and Martin R. Delaney as assistant editor, made its appearance in Rochester, New York. The prospectus stated that its object was "to attack slavery in all of its forms and aspects; advance Universal Emancipation; exact the standard of public morality; promote the moral and intellectual improvement of the colored people; and to hasten the day of freedom to our three million enslaved fellow-countrymen."

The North Star became one of the outstanding anti-slavery papers in the North and one of the very few to remain in existence over a long period of time. In 1855 it changed its name to *Frederick Douglass' Paper* and, in 1859, to *Douglass' Monthly*. But at all times during its sixteen years, the paper, edited by a man who had spent the first twenty years of his life in slavery, was proof of the potentialities of a people enthralled, and, as the *New York Tribune* pointed out, was the perfect answer to the question as to whether fugitive slaves who came North "do or do not necessarily become thieves or paupers."[15] Although few men in the Abolitionist movement spoke oftener, more effectively, or to larger audiences than did Douglass, in many ways the most effective work for emancipation was conducted through his paper. Many of his editorials were widely reprinted and reached a vast number of readers.

From the outset of his career as a journalist, Douglass was plagued by financial worries. His paper received little support from the Boston Abolitionists, against whose advice it had been launched, and more than half of the original sum of two thousand dollars advanced by his friends in England went to purchase printing materials. By March, 1849, the money was completely exhausted and Douglass was about two hundred dollars in debt.[16]

If the paper survived at all it was due to Douglass' own tireless work plus the assistance of a few devoted friends in America and England. Whenever the journal faced pressing financial difficulties, Douglass departed on a lecture tour to raise funds, supplying his readers with a detailed account of his tour by means of editorial correspondence. Gerrit Smith, a wealthy anti-slavery leader who lived in Peterboro, New York, and several other friends also came forward with contributions. Julia W. Griffiths of the Rochester Ladies Anti-Slavery Society also came to Douglass' aid, sponsoring fairs and publishing *Autographs for Freedom*, a gift book consisting of Abolitionist poems, letters, essays, and extracts from famous speeches. In an editorial in his paper, Douglass paid tribute to Miss Griffiths' support: "In referring to those who have assisted us in keeping up the paper during the year, and for the past three years, we are indebted to none more than to that ever active friend of the slave, Miss Julia Griffiths."

His knowledge of the significant role women were playing in the Abolitionist movement was an important factor in arousing Douglass' interest in the struggle for Women's Rights. A year after *The North Star* was founded, the first Women's Rights convention took place at Seneca Falls, New York. Douglass, who had featured the slogan, "Right is of no sex" in the first issue of his paper, attended the convention along with thirty-one other men courageous enough to run the risk of being branded "Hermaphrodites" and "Aunt Nancy Men." The Negro leader was the only man at the convention who was prepared to support Elizabeth Cady Stanton's resolution calling for woman suffrage* and, in a speech which helped swing many votes for the proposal, pointed out that political equality was essential for the complete liberation of women.[17] In *The North Star* of July 28, 1848, Douglass again announced his support of the "grand movement for attaining the civil, social, political, and religious rights of women," and added: "Standing as we do upon the watch-tower of human freedom, we can not be deterred from an expression of our approbation of any movement, however humble, to improve and elevate the character of any members of the human family. . . . We are free to say that in respect to political rights, we hold woman to be justly entitled to all we claim for man. . . . Our doctrine is that 'right is of no sex!' We therefore bid the women engaged in this movement our humble Godspeed."

And a few years before his death, in an address before the International Council of Women, he declared:

> "There are few facts in my humble history to which I look back with more satisfaction than to the fact, recorded in the history of the Woman Suffrage movement, that I was sufficiently enlightened at the early day, when only a few years from slavery, to support your resolution for woman suffrage. I have done very little in this world in which to glory, except this one act—and I certainly glory in that. When I ran away from slavery, it was for myself; when I advocated emancipation, it was for my people; but when I stood up for the rights of woman, self was out of the question, and I found a little nobility in the act."[18]

Few indeed were the Women's Rights conventions held during the 1850's at which Douglass was not a featured speaker and whose proceedings were not fully reported in his papers. Invariably the story of the convention would be followed by an editorial comment in support

---

*Years later a tablet was erected commemorating the occasion:
> On this spot stood the Wesleyan Chapel
> Where the first Woman's Rights Convention
>   in the World's History was held
>   July 19 and 20, 1848
> Elizabeth Cady Stanton
>   moved this resolution
>   which was seconded by Frederick Douglass
> That it was the duty of the women
>   of this country to secure to themselves
>   their sacred right
>   to the elective franchise.

of the resolutions and in which Douglass again insisted "that the only true basis of right was the capacity of individuals."

In addition to all his other activities, Douglass was also a "station master" and "conductor" for the Underground Railroad in Rochester. Frequently his fees from lectures would go to aid fugitive slaves who were often hidden in his home. His friends in Rochester were fond of relating the story of how they would see fugitives sitting on the stairs of Douglass' printing shop in the morning awaiting the arrival of the Negro editor and orator. Douglass would hide them until the evening and then arrange to have them sent to Oswego or Lewiston, or keep them overnight at his house and put them on the train to Canada in the morning.* In a period of two weeks only, he estimated that he had aided thirty fugitive slaves to escape to Canada.[19] However, he was quick to point out that his contribution was nothing compared to that of the great Negro heroine, Harriet Tubman.

> "Most that I have done," he wrote this famous conductor of the Underground Railroad, "has been in public, and I have received much encouragement. . . . You on the other hand have labored in a private way. . . . I have had the applause of the crowd. . . . While the most that you have done has been witnessed by a few trembling, scared and footsore bondmen. . . . The midnight sky and the silent stars have been the witnesses of your devotion to freedom and of your heroism."[20]

The task of writing weekly editorials for his paper was no simple one, but it compelled Douglass to study every aspect of the anti-slavery movement. Through this study he developed in maturity as a thinker and began to make original contributions to the solution of important ideological issues which confronted the Abolitionists. As he matured, he moved further and further away from the Garrisonian approach to these questions.

During the first ten years of his career as an Abolitionist, Douglass had accepted all of the doctrines of the Garrisonian school. The Garrisonians believed in Northern secession (under the slogan of "no union with the slave-holders"); they disdained using the ballot against slavery and they held that the Constitution was wholly a proslavery document and had to be scrapped entirely to defeat the slaveowners. Primarily they sought to effect their program by "moral suasion," contending that "the best weapons of the anti-slavery war-

---

*In the Samuel D. Porter Manuscripts at the University of Rochester Library there is a hastily scribbled, undated note by Douglass to Porter which reads: "Three men in peril. Am unwell. Need your help. Come at once."

fare were 'spiritual,' and mighty through God to the pulling down of strongholds."[21]

In the period 1841–1847, Douglass placed his hopes in the non-political activities of the anti-slavery societies. In a speech at the Higham Anti-Slavery Convention, in November, 1841, he exclaimed: "We ought to do just what the slaveholders don't want us to do; that is, use *moral suasion*. They care nothing about your political action, they don't dread the political movement; it is the *moral* movement, the appeal to men's sense of right, which makes them and all our opponents tremble." This emphasis on "moral suasion" as opposed to "militant abolitionism" was made clear at the National Convention of Colored Citizens held at Buffalo in 1843. Douglass took issue with Hugh Garnet, who urged the Negro slaves to strike for their liberties. "Now is the day and the hour," Garnet cried. "Rather die Freemen than live to be slaves." Douglass complained that there was "too much physical force" in Garnet's remarks, and that they would stimulate slave insurrections. That, he concluded, was what he wished "in no way to have any agency in bringing about and what we are called upon to avoid." By a vote of 19 to 18 the convention sustained Douglass' position, and the resolution in favor of "moral suasion" was adopted.[22]

It was John Brown who first caused Douglass to doubt the value of "moral suasion" as the major instrumentality for ending slavery. In 1847 he was invited to visit Brown's simple home in Springfield, Massachusetts. After dinner his host proceeded to expound his views on slavery. Brown not only condemned the institution, but added that the slaveholders "had forfeited their right to live, that the slaves had the right to gain their liberty in any way they could." He did not believe that moral suasion could ever liberate the slaves or that political action would abolish the system, and he went on to outline his plan to establish five bands of armed men in the Allegheny Mountains who would run off slaves to freedom in large numbers.

Douglass thought that Brown's plan had "much to commend it," but was still convinced that "moral suasion" would succeed in converting the entire nation, including the slave-holders, to the anti-slavery position. None the less, Brown's belief that slavery was actually a state of war profoundly impressed him. "My utterances," Douglass wrote later, "became more tinged by the color of this man's strong impressions." Two years after his visit to Brown, he astonished a Boston anti-slavery audience in Faneuil Hall with the announcement: "I should welcome the intelligence tomorrow, should it come, that the slaves had risen in the South, and that the sable arms which had been engaged in beautifying and adorning the South, were engaged in spreading death and devastation."[23] In 1852, Douglass declared that "the only way to make the Fugitive Slave Law a dead letter is to make a half-a-dozen or more dead kidnappers."[24] And in 1856 he wrote in his paper that while it was still necessary to use "persuasion and argument" and every means that promised "peacefully" to destroy slavery:

> "We feel yet that its peaceful annihilation is almost hopeless . . . and contend that the slave's right to revolt is perfect, and only wants the occurrence of favorable circumstances to become a duty. . . . Shall the millions for ever submit to robbery, to murder, to ignorance, and every unnamed evil which an irresponsible tyranny can devise, because the overthrow of that tyranny would be productive of horrors? We say not. The recoil, when it comes, will be in exact proportion to the wrongs inflicted; terrible as it will be, we accept and hope for it. . . ."[25]

During this time, under the influence of Gerrit Smith, Douglass was also growing more convinced of the weakness of the Garrisonian attitude toward the Union and the Constitution, and of the necessity for political action both for the freedom of the slaves and the improvement of the condition of free Negroes in the North. At the eighteenth annual meeting of the American Anti-Slavery Society, held at Syracuse, New York, May, 1851, a resolution was introduced to the effect that the Society would not support any paper that did not consider the Constitution a pro-slavery document. Douglass refused to support this resolution, dramatically announcing that he had reached the conclusion, after considerable thought, that the Constitution "might be consistent in its details with the noble purposes avowed in its preamble," and that it was his duty to use political as well as moral instrumentalities for the overthrow of the slave system. Enraged and amazed, Garrison cried out: "There is roguery somewhere." Douglass never forgot the remark, and from that moment the two men became estranged.[26]

In speeches and editorials Douglass developed his ideas on the character of the Constitution. The lofty lines in the Constitution's preamble that the national state had been formed to establish a more perfect union, promote the general welfare and secure the blessings of liberty, he contended, governed the meaning of the document in all its parts and details. The Constitution was thus, by its avowed purpose, anti-slavery. Slavery was not, nor could ever become, legalized, and it was the duty of the Federal government to eradicate it.

From this point Douglass moved to the next conclusion: that there was no necessity for the dissolution of the Union and that the ballot was an effective instrument for the overthrow of the slave system. He pointed out that disunion would isolate the slaves and leave them alone and helpless at the mercy of the masters. For the North to secede, as the Garrisonians frequently advocated, would have unjustly relieved it of its share of responsibility for slavery and robbed the slaves of their most important allies.

"We hear the motto 'No union with slaveholders,'" Douglass declared at an Anti-Slavery Society convention. ". . . I answer it with a more sensible motto, namely, 'No union with slaveholding.' I would unite with anybody to do right and with nobody to do wrong. I am, therefore, for drawing the bond of the Union more closely and bringing the slave states more completely under the power of the free states. What they most dread, that I most desire. The dissolution of the Union would not give the North a single advantage over slavery, but would take from it many. Within the Union we have a firm basis of opposition to slavery. Vote such men into power as will use their powers for the abolition of slavery."[27]

Douglass fully appreciated the great part that Garrison, Phillips, and other men and women of the Garrisonian school played in the Abolitionist movement. He knew that these dauntless men and women had braved the derision of the press and pulpit, faced the attacks of mobs, experienced the hardships of prison and had suffered death itself in their ceaseless struggle for the liberation of millions of Negroes in slavery. He never forgot either that it was the Garrisonians who had first discovered his potentialities to assist in that struggle, brought him before white audiences and had helped to make him an international figure. Regretfully he took issue with their theories, and only because he saw that they were dangerous to the common cause.

Once convinced of the efficacy of political action Douglass joined actively in the campaigns of the Liberty Party, to whose national committee he was appointed in 1851. Even when the Kansas-Nebraska Act repealing the Missouri Compromise created a realignment of political groups out of which emerged the Republican Party, Douglass did not abandon the independent political party of the radical Abolitionists. He was sorely disappointed at the failure of the Republican Party to call for the abolition of slavery either in the South or in the District of Columbia, and warned Abolitionists against supporting the new political movement which he characterized in June, 1856, as "a heterogeneous mass of political antagonisms, gathered from defunct Whiggery, disaffected Democracy, and demented, defeated and disappointed Native Americanism."[28]

Douglass held this view during the opening stages of the Presidential campaign of 1856, supporting Gerrit Smith, candidate of the Radical Abolitionists, for the presidency. But as the campaign progressed, his outlook changed. He realized that he could not expect a coalition of different groups within a progressive political party to accept as its platform all of the views of its most advanced section. The mass of the people were moving towards the Republican Party mainly because of their opposition to the further expansion of slavery, and no true Abolitionist could isolate himself from them. In September, 1856, therefore, Douglass announced his support of John C. Frémont, the Republican candidate for President.* Admitting that the Republican Party did not go as far as he wished it would on slavery, he pointed out that "a man was not justified in refusing to assist his fellowmen to accomplish a good thing simply because his fellows refuse to accomplish some other good thing which they deem impossible." A theory, he continued, would hardly be sound "which would prevent us from voting with men for the abolition of slavery in Maryland, simply because our companions refuse to include Virginia." Several months after the election, he again justified his *volte-face*, observing in a letter to Gerrit Smith: "We have turned Whigs and Democrats into Republicans and we can turn Republicans into Abolitionists."[29] He was soon to see his prediction fulfilled.

The most significant event in Douglass' life in the next few years before the outbreak of the Civil War was his relationship with John Brown. Early in 1858 Brown, visiting Douglass in Rochester, revealed his decision to use forceful means to free the slaves. Just what undertaking he had in mind Douglass did not at this time discover. But some months later, at Brown's request, Douglass met the "old man" in an old stone quarry at Chambersburg, Pennsylvania, about twenty miles from Harper's Ferry. Brown asked Douglass' opinion of his plan to enter Virginia, seize the arsenal at Harper's Ferry, and rouse the slaves for freedom, and appealed to Douglass to join him. The Negro leader vehemently opposed the seizing of the arsenal, urged that Brown continue the method of rescuing slaves via the underground railroad, and warned that the plan would be fatal to all involved: "It would be an attack upon the federal government and would array the whole country against us. . . . I told him . . . that all his arguments, and all descriptions of the place, convinced me that he was going into a perfect steel-trap, and that once in he would never get out alive." Brown was deeply disappointed. "I will defend you with all my life," he told Douglass. "I want you for a special purpose. When I strike, the bees will begin to swarm, and I shall want you to help me hive them."[30]

---

*Douglass, however, did not join the Republican Party. In a letter to Gerrit Smith, December 16, 1856, he wrote: "No, my Dear Sir, I am not a member of the Republican Party. I am still a radical Abolitionist." (Gerrit Smith Papers, Syracuse University Library).

On the evening of October 16, 1859, while Douglass was addressing a large audience in National Hall, Philadelphia, his speech was interrupted by the news that a party of nineteen men, fourteen white and five colored, led by Captain John Brown, had seized the Federal Arsenal at Harper's Ferry and were attempting to hold it. The next day came the report that Brown and some of his men had been captured by United States troops, and that Brown's "carpet-bag," containing letters and documents "implicating" several Abolitionists including Frederick Douglass, was in the hands of the authorities. Soon after, newspapers carried the story that "Brown has made a full statement, implicating Gerrit Smith, Joshua Giddings, and Frederick Douglass," who were promptly to be arrested "as parties implicated in the crime of murder, and as accessories before the fact."

Fearing that the federal authorities would bring him to Virginia for trial—an action which would have been tantamount to signing his death warrant—Douglass fled to Canada. Several days later the United States District Attorney for Western New York arrived in Rochester to arrest the Negro leader.

Douglass has been severely criticized by some writers for his refusal to join Brown's expedition and for having fled to Canada after the raid.[31] John E. Cook, one of the men taken with Brown, even blamed Douglass for the failure of the expedition, maintaining that the Negro orator was supposed to bring a large number of men to reinforce Brown. In a letter to the press from Canada, Douglass emphatically denied the assertion, and the evidence bears out his position.

Douglass was justified in refusing to join Brown's company. The venture, as he had told Brown, was doomed to fail. There was more work for Douglass to do than end his life at this stage on the gallows in Virginia. "It is gallant to go forth single-handed," Douglass once observed, "but is it wise?"[32] All this does not mean that he failed to grasp the significance of Brown's raid in hastening the events which led to the abolition of slavery. Douglass devoted many speeches to this theme and always paid great tribute to John Brown's courage and devotion to freedom. In an address delivered at Storer College, Harper's Ferry, in 1881, he declared:

> "But the question is: did John Brown fail? He certainly did fail to get out of Harper's Ferry before being beaten down by United States soldiers; he did fail to save his own life and to lead a liberating army into the mountains of Virginia. But he did not go to Harper's Ferry to save his life. The true question is: did John Brown draw his sword against slavery and thereby lose his life in vain? And to this I answer ten thousand times, No! . . . If John

Brown did not end the war that ended slavery, he did at least begin the war that ended slavery. If we look over the dates, places and men, for which this honor is claimed, we shall find that not Carolina, but Virginia—not Fort Sumter, but Harper's Ferry and the arsenal—not Col. Anderson [the commanding officer at Fort Sumter], but John Brown, began the war that ended American slavery and made this a free Republic. Until this blow was struck, the prospect for freedom was dim, shadowy, and uncertain. The irrepressible conflict was one of words, votes, and compromises. When John Brown stretched forth his arm the sky was cleared."[33]

Douglass had planned to visit England to raise funds for his paper and spend some time with old friends, and the aftermath of Brown's raid hastened his decision to leave. On November 12, 1859, he sailed for Liverpool. He spent most of the five months of his stay addressing meetings in England and Scotland. These anti-slavery speeches were later to bear fruit in the heroic support of the English middle and laboring classes during the Civil War.

After his return from England, Douglass devoted his time to editing his paper, campaigning for Gerrit Smith, who, in 1860, was again the Radical Abolitionists' candidate for President, and battling for Negro suffrage in New York state. Although no property qualifications existed for white voters, a Negro could not vote in the Empire State unless he owned real estate, valued at $250. As early as July, 1857, Douglass had denounced this clause.

"We ask," he declared in an address at the National Convention of Colored Men, "that an unrestricted right of suffrage, which is essential to the dignity of the white man, be extended to the colored man also."[34]

In 1860, after considerable pressure exerted by the free Negroes, the New York legislature passed an act to amend the constitution by popular vote so as to abolish the property qualifications for Negro voters. Douglass stumped the state in favor of the proposed amendment, but at the general election on November 6, 1860, it was rejected by a majority of 140,429 votes.

In this same election Abraham Lincoln was chosen President. Although Douglass did not yet regard Lincoln as a real friend of the slave, he hailed his election as a great defeat for the slave power.

"For fifty years," he wrote in the December, 1860, issue of the *Monthly*, "the country has taken the law from the lips of an exacting, haughty and imperious slave oligarchy. The masters of the slaves have been the masters of the Republic. Their authority was almost undisputed, and their power irresistible. They were the President makers of the Republic, and no aspirant dared to hope for success against their frown. Lincoln's election has vitiated their authority, and broken their power."

Douglass also saw in Lincoln's election a sign of the growing determination of the people in the North to put an end to the appeasement of the slave owners.

"Hitherto the threat of disunion has been as potent over the politicians of the North, as the cat-o'-nine-tails over the backs of the slaves. Mr. Lincoln's election breaks this enchantment, dispels this terrible nightmare, and awakes the nation to the consciousness of new powers, and the possibility of a higher destiny than the perpetual bondage to an ignoble fear."

Douglass' admiration for Lincoln mounted in the weeks following his election. He observed the President-elect's determination not to capitulate to the demands for a compromise policy that would appease secessionists and "his refusal to have concessions extorted from him under the terror instituted by thievish conspirators and traitors. . . ." The Negro editor shared Lincoln's attitude toward the pro-compromise advocates, pointing out: "All compromises now are but as new wine to old bottles, new cloth to old garments. To attempt them as means of peace between freedom and slavery, is an attempt to reverse irreversible law."[35]

After the firing upon Fort Sumter in April, 1861, Douglass became a veritable dynamo of energy. He immediately began his campaign to convince the North "that the Union cause would never prosper until the war assumed an anti-slavery attitude, and the Negro was enlisted on the loyal side." In the May, 1861, issue of his *Monthly* he featured the slogan, "Freedom for all, or Chains for all," and, in the same issue, assured Lincoln that the speediest way to secure victory was by "carrying the war into Africa." *Let the slaves and free colored people be called into service, and formed into a liberating army,* to march into the South and raise the banner of Emancipation among the slaves," he wrote in an editorial significantly entitled, "How to End the War." Although he often despaired of ever convincing Lincoln that slavery had to die that "the Union may live," Douglass continued to call upon the administration to take the proper steps to end the war. And when Lincoln, after many hesitations and delays, finally realized that national salvation was possible only by adopting the program Douglass had advocated from the outset of the war, the Negro leader rushed to support and strengthen the President. To those who doubted whether Lincoln would really carry through this program after the announcement of the preliminary Emancipation Proclamation in September, 1862, Douglass declared:

> "Abraham Lincoln may be slow . . . but Abraham Lincoln is not the man to reconsider, retract and contradict words and purposes solemnly proclaimed over his official signature. . . . No! Abraham Lincoln will take no step backward. His word has gone out over the country and the world, giving joy and gladness to the friends of freedom and progress wherever these words are read, and he will stand by them, and carry them out to the letter."[36]

Once the final Emancipation Proclamation was announced, Douglass issued flaming appeals to the Negroes, calling them to arms and urging them enlist in the Federal army. His most famous message, entitled "Men of Color to Arms," written after Governor Andrews of Massachusetts received permission from President Lincoln to recruit two Negro regiments, the 54th and 55th, was published by the leading papers of the North. He also set out to recruit one hundred men for the Negro regiment, and traveled hundreds of miles securing recruits. His sons, Charles and Lewis, were among the first to enlist.

In an article in the *Monthly* for April, 1863, Douglass gave nine reasons why a colored man should enlist. The Negro, he argued, was "either for the Government or against the Government," and just as the Union cause would be strengthened if he joined to aid the government the cause of slavery would be injured. The Negro, he continued, should learn the use of arms, for "the only way open to any race to make their rights respected is to learn how to defend them." By enlisting he would establish his right of citizenship in the country, demonstrate his courage, and recover his self respect. The enlistment of Negroes would be "one of the most certain means of preventing the country from drifting back into the whirlpool of pro-slavery compromise at the end of the war. . . ." Finally, he should enlist because "the war for the Union, whether men so call it or not, is a war for Emancipation."

> "Enlist, therefore, enlist without delay, enlist now, and put an end to the human barter and butchery which have stained the whole South with the warm blood of young people, and loaded its air with their groans. Enlist, and deserve not only well of your country, and win for yourselves, a name and a place among men, but secure to yourself what is infinitely more precious, the fast dropping tears of your kith and kin marked out for destruction, and who are but now ready to perish."

Douglass erected no conditions for the participation of the Negro in the Union army. The discrimination practiced against Negroes in the armed forces was deplorable but it must not serve as a barrier to the full participation of the Negro in the war.

"Nothing can be more plain," he declared in his famous Philadelphia recruiting speech in July, 1863, "nothing more certain than that the speediest and best possible way open to us to manhood, equal rights and elevation, is that we enter this service. For my own part, I hold that if the Government of the United States offered nothing more, as an inducement to colored men to enlist, than bare subsistence and arms, considering the moral effect of compliance upon ourselves, it would be the wisest and best thing for us to enlist."

The major issue was to win the war against slavery, and there was every assurance that just as events had forced the administration to emancipate the slaves, they would compel it to abandon many of the discriminatory practices.

"Colored men going into the army and navy," wrote Douglass in the *Monthly* of February, 1863, "must expect annoyance. They will be severely criticized and even insulted—but let no man hold back on this account. We shall be fighting a double battle, against slavery in the South and against prejudice and proscription in the North—and the case presents the very best assurances of success."

Douglass himself led in fighting this double battle. Worried over the failure of the administration to eliminate many grievances of Negro soldiers who had enlisted, he sought an interview with President Lincoln. He was cordially received at the White House; when he started to tell Lincoln who he was and what he was doing, the President stopped him, saying: "You need not tell me who you are, Mr. Douglass. I know who you are. . . ." Douglass told Lincoln that he was recruiting colored troops and, in order to insure the success of this branch of the service, the government had to give colored soldiers the same pay that white soldiers received; compel the Confederacy to treat colored soldiers, when taken prisoners, as prisoners of war; promote colored soldiers who distinguished themselves for bravery in the field precisely as white men were promoted for similar service, and retaliate in kind when any colored soldiers were murdered in cold blood.

Lincoln listened attentively and sympathetically to these proposals. The time was not yet ripe, he replied, to give Negro soldiers the same pay as a white man, for opposition to the use of Negroes in the Union army was still too strong. "I assure you, Mr. Douglass," he went on, "that in the end they shall have the same pay as white soldiers."* He agreed that Negro soldiers should be promoted for good conduct in the field, and should be treated as prisoners of war when captured. But he could not accept Douglass' suggestion for the adoption of retaliatory measures. "Once begun," he declared, "I do not know where such a measure would stop."[37]

Although the President's replies did not entirely satisfy Douglass, he "was so well satisfied with the man and with the educating tendency of the conflict" that he determined to go on recruiting.

From the White House Douglass went to visit Secretary of War Edwin M. Stanton who promised to give the Negro leader a commission as assistant adjutant on the staff of General Lorenzo Thomas, then in Mississippi. Douglass returned to Rochester and, on August 16, 1863, wrote his "Valedictory" to the "Respected Readers" of his paper. He explained that he was ceasing to publish his paper because he was "going South to assist Adjutant General Thomas, in the organization of colored troops, who shall win for the million in bondage the inestimable blessings of liberty and country."[†] But for some reason that has never been made clear, Douglass did not receive the commission promised by Secretary Stanton and, though offered a salary and expenses, refused to enter upon the undertaking. Instead he returned to the lecture platform, analyzing in his speeches the major issues confronting the nation in winning the war and securing full freedom for the Negro people.

At no time during the conflict did Douglass regard the aims of the war to be merely those of restoring the Southern states to the Union. "We are fighting for something incomparably better than the old Union," he announced as early as 1863. "We are fighting for unity of idea, unity of sentiment, unity of object, unity of institutions, in which there shall be no North, no South, no East, no West, no black, no white, but a solidarity of the nation, making every slave free, and every free man a voter."[38]

Yet even before the war ended, Douglass expressed doubt that these objectives would be easy to realize. In a speech in Faneuil Hall early in April, 1865, he observed that the Negroes were always citizens in time

---

*On July 14, 1864, Congress passed a bill granting Negro soldiers the same pay as white soldiers, retroactive to January 1, 1864.

†Douglass gave other reasons for ending the publication of his paper. "Neither do I discontinue the paper," he wrote, "because I think that speaking and writing against slavery and its twin monster prejudice against the colored race are no longer needful. Such writing and speaking will be necessary so long as slavery and proscription shall remain in this country and in the world. Happily, however, I can write now through channels which were not opened fully to these subjects, when my journal was established. . . . So that while speaking and writing are still needful, the need for a special organ for my views and opinions on slavery no longer exists." (*Douglass' Monthly*, August, 1863.)

of national trouble. What he wanted was to have the black man a citizen "all over the country not only in time of war but in time of peace," and to have his people secure the right to vote. The American people, he declared, by calling upon the Negro to take part in the war, had "bound themselves to protect the Southern Negro from all consequences that may arise from his allegiance to the Union." As he was to explain again and again, the American people owed the Negro people a debt which could only be paid by assuring the Negroes full freedom. Emancipation alone was not enough; to make it meaningful, political, economic and civil rights had to be added.

For a time Douglass had believed that after the close of the Civil War his work would be ended, and that he would be able to buy a farm and retire from public life. But he "soon found that the Negro had still a cause, and that he needed my voice and pen, with others, to plead for it." During the early months of the administration of Andrew Johnson, who became President after Lincoln's assassination, the former slaveowners regained control of the Southern state legislatures and adopted a series of laws which all but re-enslaved the Negro masses. At the same time the Federal government, following Johnson's orders, drove the Negroes off land that had been distributed to them during Lincoln's administration, and aided the planters in reducing the freedmen to a state of servitude. Landless, without citizenship, without the right to vote and civil rights, the Negro toilers were "free from the individual master, but the slave of society." Small wonder that so many freedmen cried that all that was "needed to restore slavery was the auction block and the driver's lash." Small wonder, too, that Douglass decided to abandon his plans to retire from public life, and began again to use his voice and pen for freedom's cause.

Realizing that there was little chance of improving the conditions of the freedmen until they became citizens, Douglass set to work to secure the ballot for the recently emancipated Negro masses and, in speech after speech, he sought to drive home the concept that "the general welfare of the Negro was best served by the franchise."* With

---

*For a short while after the Civil War, Douglass joined with leaders of the Woman's Rights movement in advocating the immediate granting of the ballot to both the freedmen and women. But he soon changed his stand, believing that it was impossible to secure the ballot for both groups at the same time and that the Negro more urgently needed the right to vote. Many leaders of the women's movement disagreed with him, but they never questioned his sincerity and devotion to the cause of woman's rights. Douglass never lost interest in the woman's suffrage movement. In 1885 he wrote: "I am taking much interest just now in the Woman Suffrage question, and find the meetings for this purpose a substitute for the old anti-slavery meetings." (Douglass to Oliver Johnson, Douglass mss., Frederick Douglass Memorial Home, Anacostia, D.C.)

the ballot the Negro would be bound to elevate himself, for something then would be expected of him. On the other hand, to leave him without the ballot would be "to make him the helpless victim of the resentment provoked by freeing him." To give him the ballot, however, would provide him "with a right and power which will be ever present, and will form a wall of fire for his protection." Aside from all this, the Negro had earned the ballot by rushing to the aid of the nation in its hour of distress.[39]

Early in 1866 Douglass was appointed by a Negro convention to serve on a committee to interview President Johnson on certain major issues relating to the freedmen. The delegation called at the White House on February 7, 1866, and informed Johnson that they were not content with an amendment prohibiting slavery but wanted it buttressed by appropriate legislation. Douglass told Johnson: "Your noble and humane predecessor placed in our hands the sword to assist in saving the nation, and we do hope that you, his able successor, will favorably regard the placing in our hands, the ballot with which to save ourselves." After proclaiming what a friend he was of the colored people, Johnson declared that granting the Negro the ballot would lead to a "war of races" in the South between the freedmen and the poor whites. The only way to avoid this calamity, replied Douglass, was by "the enfranchisement of the blacks." Answering Johnson's statement, that the planters would control the Negro's vote if he possessed the ballot, Douglass said: "Let the Negro once understand that he has an organic right to vote, and he will raise up a party in the Southern states among the poor, who will rally with him. There is this conflict that you speak of between the wealthy slaveowner and the poor man."

When the interview was over, Douglass, turning to leave, said: "The President sends us to the people and we go to the people."[40] The Negro delegation designated Douglass to write a reply to the various points raised by Johnson, and this document was widely published and aroused considerable public discussion. As Douglass wrote later:

> "What was said on the occasion brought the whole question virtually before the American people. Until that interview the country was not fully aware of the intentions and policy of President Johnson on the subject of reconstruction, especially in respect to the newly emancipated class of the South."

While in Washington the Negro delegation visited Congressmen and Senators and urged the passage of a law enfranchising the freedmen. When the delegation left the nation's capital, Douglass remained to continue lobbying for the measure.

In August, 1866, Douglass was appointed by the Republicans of

Rochester a delegate to the National Loyalists Convention, which was to meet in Philadelphia the following month. On the train to Philadelphia a committee sent by other delegates approached him and urged him not to attend the convention, arguing that his presence would injure the Republican Party as well as the cause of his own people. Douglass replied that they might as well ask him "to blow my brains out." The only thing the Republican Party would gain from his staying away would be a reputation "for hypocrisy and cowardice." "But ignoring the question of policy entirely," he declared, "and looking at it as one of right and wrong, I am bound to go into that convention; not to do so would contradict the principle and practice of my life."[41]

Douglass went; was welcomed at first only by General Benjamin Butler, but remained to hear himself cheered for his brilliant analysis of national issues. With Anna E. Dickinson, the remarkable woman orator, and Theodore Tilton, editor of the New York *Independent*, he fought to have the convention go on record in favor of Negro suffrage. All three criticized the delegates from the Border states for their opposition to Negro suffrage. Southerners, said Douglass, frequently told him, "Keep still; it will all come in good time; don't pile it on too heavy; don't do that; let us get out of the well and we will attend to you afterwards." "You remember the fable of the fox and the goat who were in the well together," the Negro orator continued. "The fox said he could get out by mounting the goat's horns, and then he would help the goat out. Reynard forgot the poor goat and it remained in the well still."

He asked for suffrage for the black man only because it was "his right," and he asked for it *now* because this was the time when the nation was still keenly aware of the contributions of the Negroes to the victory achieved in the Civil War. "Surely if the black man can pay taxes, he can vote. If he can use the loyal musket he can vote."[42]

On September 7, the convention thanked Anna Dickinson and Frederick Douglass for their moving addresses and adopted a report endorsing Negro suffrage. The action of the convention, Douglass pointed out later, "turned the tide of political sentiment in favor of enfranchisement. . . ."[43]

A few months after the National Loyalists Convention went on record in favor of Negro suffrage, the Radical Republican plan of Reconstruction was adopted by Congress. Douglass hailed the provisions requiring the enfranchisement of the Negro people in the South, but sorely regretted the failure to include similar guarantees to enable the freedmen to become landowners. Convinced that economic freedom was essential for the Negro toilers, he suggested the establishment of a National Land and Labor Company, capitalized at a million dollars, which would sell land on easy terms to colored people in the South. But his proposal was too radical for the industrial and financial leaders who dominated the Republican Party and was shelved. Years later Douglass pointed to the failure to provide for the economic emancipation of the freedmen as the basic flaw in the Reconstruction policies of the Republican Party.* Without economic independence, the Negro in the South was only "nominally free"; actually he was "still a slave."

"They gave the freedman the machinery of liberty but denied him the steam with which to put it into motion. They gave him the uniform of soldiers, but no arms; they called them citizens and left them subjects. . . . They did not deprive the old master class of the power of life and death which was the soul of the relation of master and slave. They could not of course sell them, but they retained the power to starve them to death, and wherever this power is held, there is the power of slavery."[44]

Even after the passage of the Radical Reconstruction program, Douglass continued to battle for the enfranchisement of the Negro people. For one thing, the Congressional Act of 1867 applied only to Negroes in the South; for another, it was still possible for state legislatures to repeal laws granting the right to vote to colored men. Hence he flung himself into the campaign for the enactment of a constitutional amendment guaranteeing Negro suffrage all over the country. Early in 1869 the fifteenth amendment was adopted. Douglass attended the celebration held in Baltimore in honor of the passage of the amendment, and heard the great assemblage adopt a resolution calling upon him to use "the power of his magnificent manhood [to] help us to a higher, broader, and nobler mankind."[45]

Until his death a quarter of a century later, Douglass did use his great abilities to help his people achieve "a higher, broader, and nobler mankind." Lecturer and editor, President of the Colored National Labor Union, Recorder of Deeds in Washington, chargé to Santo Domingo and minister resident and consul general to Haiti, he contributed his energies towards that main purpose. He fought for the dig-

---

*Although Douglass was not uncritical of the Republican Party, he continued to support the party even after it had ceased to be a progressive organization and was already the representative in the political arena of the dominant groups in American industry and finance. Like other Negro spokesmen, Douglass believed that the Democratic Party in the South was so completely reactionary on the Negro question that there was no alternative to supporting the Republicans. He did point out, however, that he was not for the Republicans "right or wrong." (See his letter in Open Court, 1893, p. 4416.)

nity of his people, always emphasizing that exploitation of and discrimination against colored people was not a Negro problem but an American problem. "No man can put a chain about the ankle of his fellow man, without at last finding the other end of it fastened about his own neck," he told the nation.[46]

"The lesson now flashed upon the attention of the American People," he once wrote, "the lesson which they must learn, or neglect to do so at their own peril, is that 'Equal Manhood means Equal Rights,' and that further, that the American people must stand each for all and all for each, without respect to color or race. . . . I expect to see the colored people of this country enjoying the same freedom, voting at the same ballot-box, using the same cartridge-box, going to the same schools, attending the same churches, traveling in the same street cars, in the same railroad cars, on the same steamboats, proud of the same country, fighting the same foe, and enjoying the same peace and all its advantages. . . ."[47]

Frederick Douglass did not live to see this hope realized. But today, a half century after his death, in the crucible of the war against fascism, the people are rapidly learning the lesson he taught—that "Equal Manhood means Equal Rights," and that they must "stand each for all and all for each, without respect to color or race." All over the world millions of men and women of all races, colors, creeds, and nationalities are moving forward together to achieve victory, enduring peace, security and freedom.

Never before in our history were the words of Frederick Douglass as significant as they are today. The war has raised the question of Negro rights in the most acute form. The vast contributions of the Negro people in our nation's war effort have made it clearer every day that we cannot achieve victory, lasting peace, and security without the Negro people, nor without satisfying their just demands. Hence we can look forward confidently to the day when Frederick Douglass' vision of complete equality for all Americans will be realized.

The writings and speeches of Frederick Douglass included in this booklet have been arranged in four sections, covering slavery, the Civil War, Reconstruction and other democratic utterances on Woman's Rights, Labor, Education, etc. Within each section the Douglass text has been preceded by headings furnished by the editor.

I. SLAVERY

What Is Slavery?

SLAVERY in the United States is the granting of that power by which one man exercises and enforces a right of property in the body and soul of another. The condition of a slave is simply that of the brute beast. He is a piece of property—a marketable commodity, in the language of the law, to be bought and sold at the will and caprice of the master who claims him to be his property; he is spoken of, thought of, and treated as property. His own good, his conscience, his intellect, his affections, are all set aside by the master. The will and the wishes of the master are the law of the slave. He is as much a piece of property as a horse. If he is fed, he is fed because he is property. If he is clothed, it is with a view to the increase of his value as property. Whatever of comfort is necessary to him for his body or soul that is inconsistent with his being property is carefully wrested from him, not only by public opinion, but by the law of the country. He is carefully deprived of everything that tends in the slightest degree to detract from his value as property. He is deprived of education. God has given him an intellect; the slaveholder declares it shall not be cultivated. If his moral perception leads him in a course contrary to his value as property, the slaveholder declares he shall not exercise it. The marriage institution cannot exist among slaves, and one-sixth of the population of democratic America is denied its privileges by the law of the land. What is to be thought of a nation boasting of its liberty, boasting of its humanity, boasting of its Christianity, boasting of its love of justice and purity, and yet having within its own borders three millions of persons denied by law the right of marriage?—what must be the condition of that people?[1]

The Slave Trade

Behold the practical operation of this internal slave-trade, the American slave-trade, sustained by American politics and American religion. Here you will see men and women reared like swine for the market. You know what is a swine-drover? I will show you a man-drover. They inhabit all our Southern states. They perambulate the country, and crowd the highways of the nation, with droves of human stock. You will see one of these human flesh jobbers, armed with pistol, whip, and bowie-knife, driving a company of a hundred men, women, and children, from the Potomac to the slave market at New Orleans. These wretched people are to be sold singly, or in lots, to suit purchasers. They are food for the cottonfield and the deadly sugar-mill. Mark the sad procession, as it moves wearily along, and the inhuman wretch who drives them. Hear his savage yells and his blood-curdling oaths, as he hurries on his affrighted captives! There, see the old man with locks thinned and gray. Cast one glance, if you please, upon that young mother, whose shoulders are bare to the scorching sun, her briny tears falling on the brow of the babe in her arms. See, too, that girl of thirteen, weeping, *yes!* weeping, as she thinks of the mother from whom she has been torn! The drove moves tardily. Heat and sorrow have nearly consumed their strength; suddenly you hear a quick snap, like the discharge of a rifle; the fetters clank, and the chain rattles simultaneously; your ears are saluted with a scream, that seems to have torn its way to the centre of your soul! The crack you heard was the sound of the slave-whip; the scream you heard was from the woman you saw with the babe. Her speed had faltered under the weight of her child and chains! That gash on her shoulder tells her to move on. Follow this drove to New Orleans. Attend the auction; see men examined like horses; see the forms of women rudely and brutally exposed to the shocking gaze of American slave-buyers. See this drove sold and separated forever; and never forget the deep, sad sobs that arose from that scattered multitude. Tell me, citizens, WHERE, under the sun, you can witness a spectacle more fiendish and shocking. Yet this is but a glance at the American slave-trade, as it exists, at this moment, in the ruling part of the United States.

I was born amid such sights and scenes. To me the American slave-trade is a terrible reality. When a child, my soul was often pierced with a sense of its horrors. I lived on Philpot Street, Fell's Point, Baltimore, and have watched from the wharves the slave ships in the Basin, anchored from the shore, with their cargoes of human flesh, waiting for favorable winds to waft them down the Chesapeake. There was, at that time, a grand slave mart kept at the head of Pratt Street, by Austin Woldfolk. His agents were sent into every town and county in Maryland, announcing their arrival, through the papers, and on flaming *"hand-bills,"* headed CASH FOR NEGROES. These men were generally well dressed men, and very captivating in their manners; ever ready to drink, to treat, and to gamble. The fate of many a slave has depended upon the turn of a single card; and many a child has been snatched from the arms of its mother by bargains arranged in a state of brutal drunkenness.

The flesh-mongers gather up their victims by dozens, and drive them, chained, to the general depot at Baltimore. When a sufficient number has been collected here, a ship is chartered for the purpose of conveying the forlorn crew to Mobile, or to New Orleans. From the slave prison to the ship, they are usually driven in the darkness of night; for since the anti-slavery agitation, a certain caution is observed.

In the deep, still darkness of midnight, I have been often aroused by the dead, heavy footsteps, and the piteous cries of the chained gangs that passed our door. The anguish of my boyish heart was intense; and I was often consoled, when speaking to my mistress in the morning, to hear her say that the custom was very wicked; that she hated to hear the rattle of the chains and the heartrending cries. I was glad to find one who sympathized with me in my horror.

Fellow-citizens, this murderous traffic is, today, in active operation in this boasted republic. In the solitude of my spirit I see clouds of dust raised on the highways of the South; I see the bleeding footsteps; I hear the doleful wail of fettered humanity on the way to the slave-markets, where the victims are to be sold like *horses, sheep,* and *swine,* knocked off to the highest bidder. There I see the tenderest ties ruthlessly broken, to gratify the lust, caprice and rapacity of the buyers and sellers of men. My soul sickens at the sight.[2]

"Is the Slave a Man?"

But I fancy I hear some one of my audience say, "It is just in this circumstance that you and your brother Abolitionists fail to make a favorable impression on the public mind. Would you argue more, and denounce less; would you persuade more, and rebuke less; your cause would be much more likely to succeed." But, I submit, where all is plain there is nothing to be argued. What point in the anti-slavery creed would you have me argue? On what branch of the subject do the people of this country need light? Must I undertake to prove that the slave is a man? That point is conceded already. Nobody doubts it. The slaveholders themselves acknowledge it in the enactment of laws for their government. They acknowledge it when they punish disobedience on the part of the slave. There are seventy-two crimes in the State of Virginia which, if committed by a black man (no matter how ignorant he be) subject him to the punishment of death; while only two of the same crimes will subject a white man to the like punishment. What is this but the acknowledgment that the slave is a moral, intellectual, and responsible being? The manhood of the slave is conceded. It is admitted in the fact that Southern statute books are covered with enactments forbidding, under severe fines and penalties, the teaching of the slave to read or to write. When you can point to any such laws in reference to the beasts of the field, then I may consent to argue the manhood of the slave. When the dogs in your streets, when the fowls of the air, when the cattle on your hills, when the fish of the sea, and the reptiles that crawl, shall be unable to distinguish the slave from a brute, *then* will I argue with you that the slave is a man!

For the present, it is enough to affirm the equal manhood of the Negro race. Is it not astonishing that, while we are ploughing, planting, and reaping, using all kinds of mechanical tools, erecting houses, constructing bridges, building ships, working in metals of brass, iron, copper, silver and gold; that, while we are reading, writing and ciphering, acting as clerks, merchants and secretaries, having among us lawyers, doctors, ministers, poets, authors, editors, orators and teachers; that, while we are engaged in all manner of enterprises common to other men, digging gold in California, capturing the whale in the Pacific, feeding sheep and cattle on the hill-side, living, moving, acting, thinking, planning, living in families as husbands, wives and children, and, above all, confessing and worshipping the Christian's God, and looking hopefully for life and immortality beyond the grave, we are called upon to prove that we are men!

What, am I to argue that it is wrong to make men brutes, to rob them of their liberty, to work them without wages, to keep them ignorant of their relations to their fellow men, to beat them with sticks, to flay their flesh with the lash, to load their limbs with irons, to hunt them with dogs, to sell them at auction, to sunder their families, to knock out their teeth, to burn their flesh, to starve them into obedience and submission to their masters? Must I argue that a system thus marked with blood, and stained with pollution, is *wrong*? No! I will not. I have better employment for my time and strength than such arguments would imply.[3]

The Effects of Slavery on the Status of Southern White Workers

The slaveholders, with a craftiness peculiar to themselves, by encouraging the enmity of the poor labouring white man against the blacks, succeeded in making the said white man almost as much a slave as the black slave himself. The difference between the white slave and the black slave was this: the latter belonged to one slaveholder, and the former belonged to the slaveholders collectively. The white slave had taken from him by indirection what the black slave had taken from him directly and without ceremony. Both were plundered, and by the same plunderers. The slave was robbed by his master of all his earnings, above what was required for his bare physical necessities, and the white labouring man was robbed by the slave system of the just results of his labour, because he was flung into competition with a class of labourers who worked without wages.[4]

Slavery is Inconsistent with Republicanism

Americans! your republican politics, not less than your republican religion, are flagrantly inconsistent. You boast of your love of liberty, your superior civilization, and your pure Christianity, while the whole political power of the nation (as embodied in the two great political parties) is solemnly pledged to support and perpetuate the enslavement of three millions of your countrymen. You hurl your anathemas at the crowned headed tyrants of Russia and Austria and pride yourselves on your Democratic institutions, while you yourselves consent to be the mere *tools and body-guards* of the tyrants of Virginia and Carolina. You invite to your shores fugitives of oppression from abroad, honor them with banquets, greet them with ovations, cheer them, toast them, salute them, protect them, and pour out your money to them like water; but the fugitives from your own land you advertise, hunt, arrest, shoot, and kill. You glory in your refinement and your universal education; yet you maintain a system as barbarous and dreadful as ever stained the character of a nation—a system begun in avarice, supported in pride, and perpetuated in cruelty. You shed tears over fallen Hungary, and make the sad story of her wrongs the theme of your poets, statesmen and orators, till your gallant sons are ready to fly to arms to vindicate her cause against the oppressor; but, in regard to the ten thousand wrongs of the American slave, you would enforce the strictest silence, and would hail him as an enemy of the nation who dares to make those wrongs the subject of public discourse! You are all on fire at the mention of liberty for France or for Ireland; but are as cold as an iceberg at the thought of liberty for the enslaved of America. You discourse eloquently on the dignity of labor; yet, you sustain a system which, in its very essence, casts a stigma upon labor. You can bare your bosom to the storm of British artillery to throw off a three-penny tax on tea; and yet wring the last hard-earned farthing from the grasp of the black laborers of your country. You profess to believe "that, of one blood, God made all nations of men to dwell on the face of all the earth," and hath commanded all men, everywhere, to love one another; yet you notoriously hate (and glory in your hatred) all men whose skins are not colored like your own. You declare before the world, and are understood by the world to declare that you *"hold these truths to be self-evident, that all*

*men are created equal; and are endowed by their Creator with certain in-
alienable rights; and that among these are, life, liberty, and the pursuit
of happiness"*; and yet, you hold securely, in a bondage which, according to your own Thomas Jefferson, *"is worse than ages of that which
your fathers rose in rebellion to oppose," a seventh part* of the inhabitants
of your country.

Fellow-citizens, I will not enlarge further on your national inconsis-
tencies. The existence of slavery in this country brands your republi-
canism as a sham, your humanity as a base pretense, and your
Christianity as a lie. It destroys your moral power abroad; it corrupts
your politicians at home. It saps the foundation of religion; it makes
your name a hissing and a bye-word to a mocking earth. It is the an-
tagonistic force in your government, the only thing that seriously dis-
turbs and endangers your *Union*. It fetters your progress; it is the enemy
of improvement; the deadly foe of education; it fosters pride; it breeds
insolence; it promotes vice; it shelters crime; it is a curse to the earth
that supports it; and yet you cling to it as if it were the sheet anchor of
all your hopes. Oh! be warned! be warned! a horrible reptile is coiled
up in your nation's bosom; the venomous creature is nursing at the tender breast of your youthful republic; *for the love of God, tear away*, and
fling from you the hideous monster, and *let the weight of twenty millions crush and destroy it forever!*[5]

What Does July Fourth Mean to the Slave?

Fellow-citizens, pardon me, allow me to ask, why am I called upon to
speak here today? What have I, or those I represent, to do with your national independence? Are the great principles of political freedom and
of natural justice, embodied in that Declaration of Independence, extended to us? and am I, therefore, called upon to bring our humble offering to the national altar, and to confess the benefits and express de-
vout gratitude for the blessings resulting from your independence to
us? . . .

What, to the American slave, is your 4th of July? I answer; a day that
reveals to him, more than all other days in the year, the gross injustice
and cruelty to which he is the constant victim. To him, your celebration is a sham; your boasted liberty, an unholy license; your national
greatness, swelling vanity; your sounds of rejoicing are empty and heart-
less; your denunciation of tyrants brass fronted impudence; your shouts
of liberty and equality, hollow mockery; your prayers and hymns, your
sermons and thanksgivings, with all your religious parade and solem-
nity, are to him, mere bombast, fraud, deception, impiety, and
hypocrisy—a thin veil to cover up crimes which would disgrace a

nation of savages. There is not a nation on the earth guilty of practices more shocking and bloody than are the people of the United States, at this very hour.

Go where you may, search where you will, roam through all the monarchies and despotisms of the Old World, travel through South America, search out every abuse, and when you have found the last, lay your facts by the side of the everyday practices of this nation, and you will say with me, that, for revolting barbarity and shameless hypocrisy, America reigns without a rival.[6]

The Negro's Right to Remain in America

I would ask you, my friends, if this is not mean and impudent in the extreme, for one class of Americans to ask for the removal of another class? I feel, sir, I have as much right in this country as any other man. I feel that the black man in this land has as much right to stay in this land as the white man. Consider the matter in the light of possession in this country. Our connection with this country is contemporaneous with your own. From the beginning of the existence of this people, as a people, the colored man has had a place upon the American soil. To be sure, he was not driven from his home in pursuit of a greater liberty than he enjoyed at home, like the Pilgrim fathers; but in the same year that the Pilgrims were landing in this State, slaves were landing on the James River, in Virginia. We feel on this score, then, that we have as much right here as any other class of people.

We have other claims to being regarded and treated as American citizens. Some of our number have fought and bled for this country, and we only ask to be treated as well as those who have fought against it. We are lovers of this country, and we only ask to be treated as well as the haters of it. . . . For my part I mean, for one, to stay in this country; I have made up my mind to live among you.[7]

There is little reason to hope that any considerable number of the free colored people will ever be induced to leave this country, even if such a thing were desirable. The black man (*un*like the Indian) loves civilization. He does not make very great progress in civilization himself, but he likes to be in the midst of it, and prefers to share its most galling evils, to encountering barbarism. Then the love of country, the dread of isolation, the lack of adventurous spirit, and the thought of seeming to desert their "brethren in bonds," are a powerful check upon all schemes of colonization, which look to the removal of the colored people, without the slaves. The truth is, dear madam [Harriet Beecher Stowe], we are *here*, and here we are likely to remain. Individuals emigrate—nations never. We have grown up with this republic, and I see nothing in her character, or even in the character of the American people, as yet, which compels the belief that we must leave the United States.[8]

I Am Proud to Be an Abolition Agitator

You sneeringly call me an "abolition agitator and ultraist." Sir, I regard this as a compliment, though you intend it as a condemnation. My only fear is, that I am unworthy of those epithets. To be an abolition agitator is simply to be one who dares to think for himself, who goes beyond the mass of mankind in promoting the cause of righteousness, who honestly and earnestly speaks out his soul's conviction, regardless of the smiles or frowns of men, leaving the pure flame of truth to burn up whatever hay, wood and stubble it may find in its way. To be such an one is the deepest and sincerest wish of my heart. It is a part of my daily prayer to God, that he will raise up and send forth more to unmask a pro-slavery church, and to rebuke a man-stealing ministry—to rock the land with agitation, and give America no peace till she repent, and be thoroughly purged of this monstrous iniquity. While Heaven lends me health and strength, and intellectual ability, I shall devote myself to this agitation; and I believe that, by so acting, I shall secure the smiles of an approving God, and the grateful approbation of my down-trodden and long abused fellow-countrymen. With these on my side, of course, I ought not to be disturbed by your displeasure, nor am I disturbed.[9]

Do the Abolitionists Undermine Religion?

Those with whom I have been laboring, namely, the old anti-slavery organization of America, have been again and again stigmatized as infidels, and for what reason? Why, solely in consequence of the faithfulness of their attacks upon the slaveholding religion of the southern states, and the northern religion that sympathizes with it. I have found it difficult to speak on this matter without persons coming forward and saying, "Douglass, are you not afraid of injuring the cause of Christ? You do not desire to do so, we know; but are you not undermining religion?" This has been said to me again and again, even since I came to this country, but I cannot be induced to leave off these exposures. I love the religion of our blessed Savior. I love that religion that comes from above, in the "wisdom of God, which is first pure, then peaceable, gentle, and easy to be entreated, full of mercy and good fruits, without partiality and without hypocrisy." I love that religion that sends its votaries to bind up the wounds of him that has fallen among thieves. I love that religion that makes it the duty of its disciples to visit the fatherless and the widow in their affliction. I love that religion that is based upon the glorious principle, of love to God and love to man; which makes its followers do unto others as they themselves would be done by. If you demand liberty to yourself, it says, grant it to your neighbors. If you claim a right to think for yourself, it says, allow your neighbors the same right. If you claim to act for yourself, it says, allow your neighbors the same right. It is because I love this religion that I hate the slaveholding, the woman-whipping, the mind-darkening, the soul-destroying religion that exists in the southern states of America. It is because I regard the one as good, and pure, and holy, that I cannot but regard the other as bad, corrupt, and wicked. Loving the one I must hate the other; holding to the one I must reject the other.[10]

What Have the Abolitionists Accomplished?

The Abolitionists of the United States have been laboring, during the last fifteen years, to establish the conviction throughout that country that slavery is a sin, and ought to be treated as such by all professing Christians. This conviction they have written about, they have spoken about, they have published about—they have used all the ordinary facilities for forwarding this view of the question of slavery. Previous to that operation, slavery was not regarded as a sin. It was spoken of as an evil—in some cases it was spoken of as a wrong—in some cases it was spoken of as an excellent institution—and it was nowhere, or scarcely anywhere, counted as a sin, or treated as a sin, except by the Society of Friends, and by the Reformed Presbyterians, two small bodies of Christians in the United States. The Abolitionists, for advocating or attempting to show that slaveholding is a sin, have been called incendiaries and madmen, and they have been treated as such—only much worse, in many instances; for they have been mobbed, beaten, pelted, and defamed in every possible way, because they disclaimed the idea that slavery is not a sin—a sin against God, a violation of the rights of man, a sin demanding immediate repentance on the part of the slaveholders, and demanding the immediate Emancipation of the trampled and down-crushed slave. They had made considerable progress in establishing this view of the case in the United States. They had succeeded in establishing, to a considerable extent, in the northern part of the United States, a deep conviction that to hold human beings in the condition of slavery is a sin, and ought to be treated as such, and that the slaveholder ought to be treated as a sinner. They had called upon the religious organizations of the land to treat slaveholding as sin. They

had recommended that the slaveholder should receive the same treatment from the church that is meted out to the ordinary thief. They had
demanded his exclusion from the churches, and some of the largest de-
nominations in the country had separated at Mason and Dixon's line,
dividing the free states from the slave states, solely on account of slaveholding, as those who hold anti-slavery views felt that they could not
stand in fellowship with men who trade in the bodies and souls of their
fellowmen.[11]

The Constitution, the Union, and Slavery

Its [the Constitution's] language is, "We the people"; not we the white
people, not even we the citizens, not we the privileged class, not we the
high, not we the low, but we the people; not we the horses, sheep, and
swine, and wheelbarrows, but we the people, we the human inhabitants; and if Negroes are people, they are included in the benefits for
which the Constitution of America was ordained and established. But
how dare any man who pretends to be the friend to the Negro thus gra-
tuitously concede away what the Negro has a right to claim under the
Constitution? Why should such friends invent new arguments to
increase the hopelessness of his bondage? This, I undertake to say, as
the conclusion of the whole matter, that the constitutionality of slavery
can be made out only by disregarding the plain and common-sense
reading of the Constitution itself; by disregarding and casting away as
worthless the most beneficent rules of legal interpretation; by ruling
the Negro outside of these beneficent rules; by claiming everything for
slavery; by denying everything for freedom; by assuming that the
Constitution does not mean what it says, and that it says what it does
not mean; by disregarding the written Constitution, and interpreting it
in the light of a secret understanding. It is in this mean, contemptible,
and underhand method that the American Constitution is pressed into
the service of slavery. They go everywhere else for proof that the
Constitution is pro-slavery but to the Constitution itself. The
Constitution declares that no person shall be deprived of life, liberty, or
property, without due process of law; it secures to every man the right
of trial by jury, the privilege of the writ of *habeas corpus*—that great writ
that put an end to slavery and slave-hunting in England; it secures to
every State a republican form of government. Any one of these provisions in the hands of Abolition Statesmen, and backed up by a right
moral sentiment, would put an end to slavery in America. . . .

The way to abolish slavery in America is to vote such men into
power, as will use their power for the abolition of slavery.

. . . My argument against the dissolution of the American Union is this: It would place the slave system more exclusively under the control of the slaveholding States, and withdraw it from the power in the Northern States which is opposed to slavery. Slavery is essentially barbarous in its character. It, above all things else, dreads the presence of an advanced civilization. It flourishes best where it meets no reproving frowns, and hears no condemning voices. While in the Union it will meet with both. Its hope of life in the last resort is to get out of the Union. I am, therefore, for drawing the bond of the Union more closely, and bringing the slave States more completely under the power of the free States. What they most dread, that I most desire. I have much confidence in the instincts of the slaveholders. They see, moreover, that if there is once a will in the people of America to abolish slavery, there is no word, no syllable in the Constitution to forbid the result. They see that the Constitution has not saved slavery in Rhode Island, in Connecticut, in New York, or Pennsylvania; that the free States have increased from one to eighteen in number, while the slave States have only added three to their original number. There were twelve slave States at the beginning of the Government; there are fifteen now. There was one free State at the beginning of the Government: there are eighteen now. The dissolution of the Union would not give the North a single advantage over slavery, but would take from it many. Within the Union we have a firm basis of opposition to slavery. It is opposed to all the great objects of the Constitution. The dissolution of the Union is not only an unwise but a cowardly measure—fifteen millions running away from three hundred and fifty thousand slaveholders. Mr. Garrison and his friends tell us that while in the Union we are responsible for slavery. He and they sing out "No union with slaveholders," and refuse to vote. I admit our responsibility for slavery while in the Union; but I deny that going out of the Union would free us from that responsibility. . . .

Its [American Anti-Slavery Society] doctrine of "No union with slaveholders," carried out, dissolves the Union, and leaves the slaves and their masters to fight their own battles, in their own way. This I hold to be an abandonment of the great idea with which that Society started. It started to free the slave. It ends by leaving the slave to free himself. It started with the purpose to imbue the heart of the nation with sentiments favorable to the abolition of slavery, and ends, by seeking to free the North from all responsibility for slavery, other than if slavery were in Great Britain, or under some other nationality. This, I say, is the practical abandonment of the idea with which that Society started.

. . . But this is not the worse fault of this Society. Its chief energies are expended in confirming the opinion, that the United States

Constitution is, and was, intended to be a slaveholding instrument—
thus piling up, between the slave and his freedom, the huge work of the
abolition of the Government, as an indispensable condition to
Emancipation. My point here is, first, the Constitution is, according to
its reading, an anti-slavery document; and, secondly, to dissolve the
Union, as a means to abolish slavery, is about as wise as it would be to
burn up this city, in order to get the thieves out of it. But again we hear
the motto, "No union with slaveholders"; and I answer it, as that noble
champion of liberty, N. P. Rogers, answered it with a more sensible
motto, namely—"No union with slaveholding." I would unite with anybody to do right, and with nobody to do wrong. And as the Union,
under the Constitution, requires me to do nothing which is wrong, and
gives me many facilities for doing good, I cannot go with the American
Anti-Slavery Society in its doctrine of disunion.[12]

Will the Slaveowners Succeed?

To the inquiry, will our enemies prevail in the execution of their de-
signs, in my God and in my soul, I believe they will not. Let us look at
the first object sought for by the slavery party of the country, *viz*: the
suppression of anti-slavery discussion. They desire to suppress discussion on this subject, with a view to the peace of the slaveholder and the
security of slavery. Now, sir, neither the principle nor the subordinate
objects here declared can be at all gained by the slave power, and for
this reason: It involves the proposition to padlock the lips of the whites,
in order to secure the fetters on the limbs of the blacks. The right of
speech, precious and priceless, cannot, will not, be surrendered to slavery. Its suppression is asked for, as I have said, to give peace and security to slaveholders. Sir, that thing cannot be done. God has interposed
an insuperable obstacle to any such result. "There can be no peace,
saith my God, to the wicked." Suppose it were possible to put down this
discussion, what would it avail the guilty slaveholder, pillowed as he is
upon the heaving bosoms of ruined souls? He could not have a peace-
ful spirit.

If every anti-slavery tongue in the nation were silent—every anti-
slavery organization dissolved—every anti-slavery press demolished—
every anti-slavery periodical, paper, book, pamphlet, or what not, were
searched out, gathered together, deliberately burned to ashes, and their
ashes given to the four winds of heaven, still, still the slaveholder could
have "no peace." In every pulsation of his heart, in every throb of his
life, in every glance of his eye, in the breeze that soothes, and in the
thunder that startles, would be waked up an accuser, whose cause is,
"Thou art, verily, guilty concerning thy brother."[13]

No Progress Without Struggle!

Let me give you a word of the philosophy of reforms. The whole history of the progress of human liberty shows that all concessions, yet made to her august claims, have been born of earnest struggle. The conflict has been exciting, agitating, all-absorbing, and for the time being putting all other tumults to silence. It must do this or it does nothing. If there is no struggle, there is no progress. Those who profess to favor freedom, and yet depreciate agitation, are men who want crops without plowing up the ground. They want rain without thunder and lightning. They want the ocean without the awful roar of its many waters. This struggle may be a moral one; or it may be a physical one; or it may be both moral and physical; but it must be a struggle. Power concedes nothing without a demand. It never did, and it never will. Find out just what people will submit to, and you have found out the exact amount of injustice and wrong which will be imposed upon them; and these will continue till they are resisted with either words or blows, or with both. The limits of tyrants are prescribed by the endurance of those whom they oppress. In the light of these ideas, Negroes will be hunted at the North, and held and flogged at the South, so long as they submit to those devilish outrages, and make no resistance, either moral or physical. Men may not get all they pay for in this world; but they must certainly pay for all they get. If we ever get free from all the oppressions and wrongs heaped upon us, we must pay for their removal. We must do this by labor, by suffering, by sacrifice, and, if needs be, by our lives, and the lives of others.[14]

II. THE CIVIL WAR

How to End the War

TO OUR mind, there is but one easy, short and effectual way to suppress and put down the desolating war which the slaveholders and their rebel minions are now waging against the American Government and its loyal citizens. Fire must be met with water, darkness with light, and war for the destruction of liberty must be met with war for the destruction of slavery. *The simple way, then, to put an end to the savage and desolating war now waged by the slaveholders, is to strike down slavery itself,* the primal cause of that war.

Freedom to the slave should now be proclaimed from the Capitol, and should be above the smoke and fire of every battle field, waving from every battle field, waving from every flag. . . . LET THE SLAVES AND FREE COLORED PEOPLE BE CALLED INTO SERVICE, AND FORMED INTO A LIBERATING ARMY, to march into the South and raise the banner of Emancipation among the slaves. . . . We have no hesitation in saying that ten thousand black soldiers might be raised in the next ten days to march upon the South. One black regiment alone would be, in such a war, the full equal of two white ones. The very fact of color in this case would be more terrible than powder and balls. The slave would learn more as to the nature of the conflict from the presence of one such regiment, than from a thousand preachers. Every consideration of justice, humanity and sound policy confirms the wisdom of calling upon black men just now to take up arms in behalf of their country.[1]

From the first, I, for one, saw in this war the end of slavery; and truth requires me to say that my interest in the success of the North was largely due to this belief. True it is that this faith was many times shaken by passing events, but never destroyed.

When Secretary Seward instructed our ministers to say to the governments to which they were accredited that, "terminate however it might, the status of no class of the people of the United States would be changed by the rebellion—that the slaves would be slaves still, and that the masters would be masters still"—when General McClellan and General Butler warned the slaves in advance that "if any attempt was made by them to gain their freedom it would be suppressed with an iron hand"—when the government persistently refused to employ Negro troops—when the Emancipation Proclamation of General John C. Fremont, in Missouri, was withdrawn—when slaves were being returned from our lines to their masters—when Union soldiers were stationed about the farm-houses of Virginia to guard and protect the master in holding his slaves—when Union soldiers made themselves more active in kicking Negro men out of their camps than in shooting rebels—when even Mr. Lincoln could tell the poor Negro that "he was the cause of the war," I still believed, and spoke as I believed, all over the North, that *the mission of the war was the liberation of the slave, as well as the salvation of the Union.*

Hence from the first I reproached the North that they fought the rebels with only one hand, when they might strike effectually with two—that they fought with their soft white hand, while they kept their black iron hand chained and helpless behind them—that they fought the effect, while they protected the cause, and that the Union cause would never prosper till the war assumed an Anti-Slavery attitude, and the Negro was enlisted on the loyal side.

In every way possible in the columns of my paper and on the platform, by letters to friends, at home and abroad, I did all that I could to impress this conviction upon this country. But nations seldom listen to advice from individuals, however reasonable. They are taught less by theories than by facts and events.

There was much that could be said against making the war an Abolition war—much that seemed wise and patriotic. "Make the war an Abolition war," we were told, "and you drive the border States into the rebellion, and thus add power to the enemy and increase the number you will have to meet on the battlefield. You will exasperate and intensify Southern feeling, making it more desperate, and put far away the day of peace between the two sections." "Employ the arm of the Negro, and the loyal men of the North will throw down their arms and go home." "This is the white man's country and the white man's war." "It would inflict an intolerable wound upon the pride and spirit of white soldiers of the Union to see the Negro in the United States uniform. Besides, if you make the Negro a soldier, you cannot depend on his courage; a crack of his old master's whip will send him scampering in terror from the field."

And so it was that custom, pride, prejudice, and the old-time respect for Southern feeling, held back the government from an Anti-Slavery policy and from arming the Negro.

Meanwhile the rebellion availed itself of the Negro most effectively. He was not only the stomach of the rebellion, by supplying its commissary department, but he built its forts, dug its entrenchments and performed other duties of the camp which left the rebel soldier more free to fight the loyal army than he could otherwise have been. It was the cotton and corn of the Negro that made the rebellion sack stand on end and caused a continuance of the war. "Destroy these," was the burden of all my utterances during this part of the struggle, "and you cripple and destroy the rebellion."[2]

When first the rebel cannon shattered the walls of Sumter and drove away its starving garrison, I predicted that the war then and there inaugurated would not be fought out entirely by white men. Every month's experience during these weary years has confirmed that opinion. A war undertaken and brazenly carried on for the perpetual enslavement of colored men, calls logically and loudly for colored men to help suppress it. Only a moderate share of sagacity was needed to see that the arm of the slave was the best defense against the arm of the slaveholder. Hence, with every reverse to the national arms, with every exulting shout of victory raised by the slaveholding rebels, I have implored the imperiled nation to unchain against her foes her powerful black hand.

Slowly and reluctantly that appeal is beginning to be heeded. Stop not now to complain that it was not heeded sooner. That it should not, may or may not have been best. This is not the time to discuss that question. Leave it to the future. When the war is over, the country saved, peace established and the black man's rights are secured, as they will be, history with an impartial hand will dispose of that and sundry other questions. Action! action! not criticism, is the plain duty of this hour. Words are now useful only as they stimulate to blows. The office of speech now is only to point out when, where, and how to strike to the best advantage.

There is no time to delay. The tide is at its flood that leads on to fortune. From East to West, from North to South, the sky is written all over, "NOW OR NEVER." "Liberty won by white men would lose half its luster." "Who would be free themselves must strike the blow." "Better even die free, than to live slaves." This is the sentiment of every brave colored man amongst us.

There are weak and cowardly men in all nations. We have them amongst us. They tell you this is the "white man's war"; that you "will be no better off after than before the war"; that the getting of you into the army is to "sacrifice you on the first opportunity." Believe them not; cowards themselves, they do not wish to have their cowardice shamed by your brave example. Leave them to their timidity, or to whatever motive may hold them back.

I have not thought lightly of the words I am now addressing you. The counsel I give comes of close observation of the great struggle now in progress, and of the deep conviction that this is your hour and mine. In good earnest, then, and after the best deliberation, I now, for the first time during this war, feel at liberty to call and counsel you to arms.

By every consideration which binds you to your enslaved fellow-countrymen and to the peace and welfare of your country; by every aspiration which you cherish for the freedom and equality of yourselves and your children; by all the ties of blood and identity which make us one with the brave black men now fighting our battles in Louisiana and in South Carolina, I urge you to fly to arms, and smite with death the power that would bury the government and your liberty in the same hopeless grave.

I wish I could tell you that the State of New York calls you to this high honor. For the moment her constituted authorities are silent on the subject. They will speak by and by, and doubtless on the right side; but we are not compelled to wait for her. We can get at the throat of treason and slavery through the State of Massachusetts. She was first in the War of Independence; first to break the chains of her slaves; first to make the black man equal before the law; first to admit colored children to her common schools, and she was first to answer with her blood the alarm-cry of the nation, when its capital was menaced by rebels. You know her patriotic governor, and you know Charles Sumner. I need not add more.

Massachusetts now welcomes you to arms as soldiers. She has but a small colored population from which to recruit. She has full leave of the general government to send one regiment to the war, and she has undertaken to do it. Go quickly and help fill up the first colored regiment from the North. I am authorized to assure you that you will receive the same wages, the same rations, the same equipments, the same protection, the same treatment, and the same bounty, secured to white soldiers. You will be led by able and skillful officers, men who will take especial pride in your efficiency and success. They will be quick to accord to you all the honor you shall merit by your valor, and to see that your rights and feelings are respected by other soldiers. I have assured myself on these points, and can speak with authority.

More than twenty years of unswerving devotion to our common cause may give me some humble claim to be trusted at this momentous crisis. I will not argue. To do so implies hesitation and doubt, and you do not hesitate. You do not doubt. The day dawns; the morning star is bright upon the horizon! The iron gate of our prison stands half open. One gallant rush from the North will fling it wide open, while four millions of our brothers and sisters shall march out into liberty.

The chance is now given you to end in a day the bondage of centuries, and to rise in one bound from social degradation to the place of common equality with all other varieties of men.

Remember Denmark Vesey of Charleston; remember Nathaniel Turner of South Hampton; remember Shields Green and Copeland, who followed noble John Brown, and fell as glorious martyrs for the cause of the slave. Remember that in a contest with oppression, the Almighty has no attribute which can take sides with oppressors.

The case is before you. This is our golden opportunity. Let us accept it, and forever wipe out the dark reproaches unsparingly hurled against us by our enemies. Let us win for ourselves the gratitude of our country, and the best blessings of our posterity through all time. The nucleus of this first regiment is now in camp at Readville, a short distance from Boston. I will undertake to forward to Boston all persons adjudged fit to be mustered into the regiment, who shall apply to me at any time within the next two weeks.[3]

Should the Negro Enlist in the Union Army?

I propose to look at the subject in a plain and practical common-sense light. There are obviously two views to be taken of such enlistments — a broad view and a narrow view. I am willing to take both, and consider both. The narrow view of this subject is that which respects the matter of dollars and cents. There are those among us who say they are in favor of taking a hand in the tremendous war, but they add they wish to do so on terms of equality with white men. They say if they enter the service, endure all hardships, perils and suffering — if they make bare their breasts, and with strong arms and courageous hearts confront rebel cannons, and wring victory from the jaws of death, they should have the same pay, the same rations, the same bounty, and the same favorable conditions every way afforded to other men.

I shall not oppose this view. There is something deep down in the soul of every man present which assents to the justice of the claim thus made and honors the manhood and self-respect which insists upon it. I say at once, in peace and in war, I am content with nothing for the black man short of equal and exact justice. The only question I have, and the point at which I differ from those who refuse to enlist, is whether the colored man is more likely to obtain justice and equality while refusing to assist in putting down this tremendous rebellion than he would be if he should promptly, generously and earnestly give his hand and heart to the salvation of the country in this its day of calamity and peril. Nothing can be more plain, nothing more certain than that the speediest and best possible way open to us to manhood, equal rights and elevation, is that we enter this service. For my own part, I hold that if the Government of the United States offered nothing more, as an inducement to colored men to enlist, than bare subsistence and arms, considering the moral effect of compliance upon ourselves, it would be the wisest and best thing for us to enlist. There is something ennobling in the possession of arms, and we of all other people in the world stand in need of their ennobling influence.

The case presented in the present war, and the light in which every colored man is bound to view it, may be stated thus. There are two governments struggling now for the possession of and endeavoring to bear rule over the United States—one has its capital in Richmond, and is represented by Mr. Jefferson Davis, and the other has its capital at Washington, and is represented by "Honest Old Abe." These two governments are today face to face, confronting each other with vast armies, and grappling each other upon many a bloody field, North and South, on the banks of the Mississippi, and under the shadows of the Alleghenies. Now, the question for every colored man is, or ought to be, what attitude is assumed by these respective governments and armies towards the rights and liberties of the colored race in this country; which is for us, and which against us!

Now, I think there can be no doubt as to the attitude of the Richmond or Confederate Government. Wherever else there has been concealment, here all is frank, open, and diabolically straightforward. Jefferson Davis and his government make no secret as to the cause of this war, and they do not conceal the purpose of the war. That purpose is nothing more or less than to make the slavery of the African race universal and perpetual on this continent. It is not only evident from the history and logic of events, but the declared purpose of the atrocious war now being waged against the country. Some, indeed, have denied that slavery has anything to do with the war, but the very same men who do this affirm it in the same breath in which they deny it, for they tell you that the Abolitionists are the cause of the war. Now, if the Abolitionists are the cause of the war, they are the cause of it only because they have sought the abolition of slavery. View it in any way you please, therefore, the rebels are fighting for the existence of slavery— they are fighting for the privilege, and horrid privilege, of sundering the dearest ties of human nature—of trafficking in slaves and the souls of men—for the ghastly privilege of scourging women and selling innocent children.

I say this is not the concealed object of the war, but the openly confessed and shamelessly proclaimed object of the war. Vice-President Stephens has stated, with the utmost clearness and precision, the difference between the fundamental ideas of the Confederate

Government and those of the Federal Government. One is based upon the idea that colored men are an inferior race, who may be enslaved and plundered forever and to the heart's content of any men of a different complexion, while the Federal Government recognizes the natural and fundamental equality of all men.

I say, again, we all know that this Jefferson Davis government holds out to us nothing but fetters, chains, auction-blocks, bludgeons, branding-irons, and eternal slavery and degradation. If it triumphs in this contest, woe, woe, ten thousand woes, to the black man! Such of us as are free, in all the likelihoods of the case, would be given over to the most excruciating tortures, while the last hope of the long-crushed bondman would be extinguished forever.

Now, what is the attitude of the Washington government towards the colored race? What reason have we to desire its triumph in the present contest? Mind, I do not ask what was its attitude towards us before this bloody rebellion broke out. I do not ask what was its disposition when it was controlled by the very men who are now fighting to destroy it when they could no longer control it. I do not even ask what it was two years ago, when McClellan shamelessly gave out that in a war between loyal slaves and disloyal masters, he would take the side of the masters against the slaves—when he openly proclaimed his purpose to put down slave insurrections with an iron hand—when glorious Ben. Butler, now stunned into a conversion to anti-slavery principles (which I have every reason to believe sincere), proffered his services to the Governor of Maryland, to suppress a slave insurrection, while treason ran riot in that State, and the warm, red blood of Massachusetts soldiers still stained the pavements of Baltimore.

I do not ask what was the attitude of this government when many of the officers and men who had undertaken to defend it openly threatened to throw down their arms and leave the service if men of color should step forward to defend it, and be invested with the dignity of soldiers. Moreover, I do not ask what was the position of this government when our loyal camps were made slave-hunting grounds, and United States officers performed the disgusting duty of slave dogs to hunt down slaves for rebel masters. There were all the dark and terrible days for the republic. I do not ask you about the dead past. I bring you to the living present. Events more mighty than men, eternal Providence, all-wise and all-controlling, have placed us in new relations to the government and the government to us. What that government is to us today, and what it will be tomorrow, is made evident by a very few facts. Look at them, colored men. Slavery in the District of Columbia is abolished forever; slavery in all the territories of the United States is abolished forever; the foreign slave trade, with its ten thousand revolting abominations, is rendered impossible; slavery in ten States of the Union is abolished forever; slavery in the five remaining States is as certain to follow the same fate as the night is to follow the day. The independence of Haiti is recognized; her Minister sits beside our Prime Minister, Mr. Seward, and dines at his table in Washington, while colored men are excluded from the cars in Philadelphia; showing that a black man's complexion in Washington, in the presence of the Federal Government, is less offensive than in the city of brotherly love. Citizenship is no longer denied us under this government.

Under the interpretation of our rights by Attorney General Bates, we are American citizens. We can import goods, own and sail ships, and travel in foreign countries with American passports in our pockets; and now, so far from there being any opposition, so far from excluding us from the army as soldiers, the President at Washington, the Cabinet and the Congress, the generals commanding and the whole army of the nation unite in giving us one thunderous welcome to share with them in the honor and glory of suppressing treason and upholding the star-spangled banner. The revolution is tremendous, and it becomes us as wise men to recognize the change, and to shape our action accordingly.

I hold that the Federal Government was never, in its essence, anything but an anti-slavery government. Abolish slavery tomorrow, and not a sentence or syllable of the Constitution need be altered. It was purposely so framed so to give no claim, no sanction to the claim of property in man. If in its origin slavery had any relation to the government, it was only as the scaffolding to the magnificent structure, to be removed as soon as the building was completed. There is in the Constitution no East, no West, no North, no South, no black, no white, no slave, no slaveholder, but all are citizens who are of American birth.

Such is the government, fellow-citizens, you are now called upon to uphold with your arms. Such is the government that you are called upon to cooperate with in burying rebellion and slavery in a common grave. Never since the world began was a better chance offered to a long enslaved and oppressed people. The opportunity is given us to be men. With one courageous resolution we may blot out the handwriting of ages against us. Once let the black man get upon his person the brass letters U.S.; let him get an eagle on his button, and a musket on his shoulder, and bullets in his pocket, and there is no power on the earth or under the earth which can deny that he has earned the right of citizenship in the United States. I say again, this is our chance, and woe betide us if we fail to embrace it. The immortal bard hath told us:

> There is a tide in the affairs of men,
> Which, taken at the flood, leads on to fortune.

Omitted, all the voyage of their life
Is bound in shallows and in miseries.
We must take the current when it serves,
Or lose our ventures.

Do not flatter yourselves, my friends, that you are more important to the government than the government is to you. You stand but as the plank to the ship. This rebellion can be put down without your help. Slavery can be abolished by white men; but liberty so won for the black man, while it may leave him an object of pity, can never make him an object of respect.

Depend upon it, this is no time for hesitation. Do you say you want the same pay that white men get? I believe that the justice and magnanimity of your country will speedily grant it. But will you be overnice about this matter? Do you get as good wages now as white men get by staying out of the service? Don't you work for less every day than white men get? You know you do. Do I hear you say you want black officers? Very well, and I have not the slightest doubt that in the progress of this war we shall see black officers, black colonels, and generals even. But is it not ridiculous in us in all at once refusing to be commanded by white men in time of war, when we are everywhere commanded by white men in time of peace? Do I hear you say still that you are a son, and want your mother provided for in your absence?—a husband, and want your wife cared for?—a brother, and want your sister secured against want? I honor you for your solicitude. Your mothers, your wives, and your sisters ought to be cared for, and an association of gentlemen, composed of responsible white and colored men, is now being organized in this city for this very purpose.

Do I hear you say you offered your services to Pennsylvania and were refused? I know it. But what of that? The State is not more than the nation. The greater includes the lesser. Because the State refuses, you should all the more readily turn to the United States. When the children fall out, they should refer their quarrel to the parent. "You came unto your own, and your own received you not." But the broad gates of the United States stand open night and day. Citizenship in the United States will, in the end, secure your citizenship in the State.

Young men of Philadelphia, you are without excuse. The hour has arrived, and your place is in the Union army. Remember that the musket—the United States musket with its bayonet of steel—is better than all mere parchment guarantees of liberty. In your hands that musket means liberty; and should your constitutional rights at the close of this war be denied, which in the nature of things, it cannot be, your brethren are safe while you have a Constitution which proclaims your right to keep and bear arms.[4]

On Abraham Lincoln

In all my interviews with Mr. Lincoln I was impressed with his entire freedom from popular prejudice against the colored race. He was the first great man that I talked with in the United States freely, who in no single instance reminded me of the difference between himself and myself, of the difference of color, and I thought that all the more remarkable because he came from a State where there were black laws. I account partially for his kindness to me because of the similarity with which I had fought my way up, we both starting at the lowest round of the ladder. . . .

There was one thing concerning Lincoln that I was impressed with, and that was that a statement of his was an argument more convincing than any amount of logic. He had a happy faculty of stating a proposition, of stating it so that it needed no argument. It was a rough kind of reasoning, but it went right to the point. Then, too, there was another feeling that I had with reference to him, and that was that while I felt in his presence that I was in the presence of a very great man, as great as the greatest, I felt as though I could go and put my hand on his shoulder. Of course I did not do it, but I felt that I could. I felt that I was in the presence of a big brother, and that there was safety in his atmosphere.[5]

All Honor to the Union Soldier

But we are not here to applaud manly courage, save as it has been displayed in a noble cause. We must never forget that victory to the rebellion meant death to the Republic. We must never forget that the loyal soldiers who rest beneath this sod flung themselves between the nation and the nation's destroyers. . . . If now we have a united country, no longer cursed by the hell-black system of human bondage, if the American name is no longer a by-word and a hissing to a mocking earth, if the star-spangled banner floats only over free American citizens in every quarter of the land, and our country has before it a long and glorious career of justice, liberty, and civilization, we are indebted to the unselfish devotion of the noble army who rest in these honored graves all around us.[6]

III. RECONSTRUCTION

Suffrage for the Negro

I HAVE had but one idea for the last three years, to present to the American people, and the phraseology in which I clothe it is the old abolition phraseology. I am for the "immediate, unconditional, and universal" enfranchisement of the black man, in every State in the Union. Without this, his liberty is a mockery; without this, you might as well almost retain the old name of slavery for his condition; for, in fact, if he is not the slave of the individual master, he is the slave of society, and holds his liberty as a privilege, not as a right. He is at the mercy of the mob, and has no means of protecting himself.

It may be objected, however, that this pressing of the Negro's right to suffrage is premature. Let us have slavery abolished, it may be said, let us have labor organized, and then, in the natural course of events, the right of suffrage will be extended to the Negro. I do not agree with this. The constitution of the human mind is such, that if it once disregards the conviction forced upon it by a revelation of truth, it requires the exercise of a higher power to produce the same conviction afterwards. The American people are now in tears. The Shenandoah has run blood—the best blood of the North. All around Richmond, the blood of New England and of the North has been shed—of your sons, your brothers and your fathers. We all feel, in the existence of this Rebellion, that judgments, terrible, widespread, far-reaching, overwhelming, are abroad in the land; and we feel, in view of these judgments, just now, a disposition to learn righteousness. This is the hour. Our streets are in mourning, tears are falling at every fireside, and under the chastisement of this Rebellion we have almost come up to the point of conceding this great, this all-important right of suffrage. I fear that if we fail to do it now, if Abolitionists fail to press it now, we may not see, for centuries to come, the same disposition that exists at this moment. Hence, I say, now is the time to press this right.

It may be asked, "Why do you want it? Some men have got along

very well without it. Women have not this right." Shall we justify one
wrong by another? This is a sufficient answer. Shall we at this moment
justify the deprivation of the Negro of the right to vote, because some
one else is deprived of that privilege? I hold that women, as well as
men, have the right to vote, and my heart and my voice go with the
movement to extend suffrage to woman; but that question rests upon
another basis than that on which our right rests. We may be asked, I
say, why we want it. I will tell you why we want it. We want it because
it is our *right*, first of all. No class of men can, without insulting their
own nature, be content with any deprivation of their rights. We want
it, again, as a means of educating our race. Men are so constituted that
they derive their conviction of their own possibilities largely from the
estimate formed of them by others. If nothing is expected of a people,
that people will find it difficult to contradict that expectation. By de-
priving us of suffrage, you affirm our incapacity to form an intelligent
judgment respecting public men and public measures; you declare
before the world that we are unfit to exercise the elective franchise,
and by this means lead us to undervalue ourselves, to put a low estimate upon ourselves, and to feel that we have no possibilities like
other men. Again, I want the elective franchise, for one, as a colored
man, because ours is a peculiar government, based upon a peculiar
idea, and that idea is universal suffrage. If I were in a monarchical government, or an autocratic or aristocratic government, where the few
bore rule and the many were subject, there would be no special stigma
resting upon me, because I did not exercise the elective franchise. It
would do me no great violence. Mingling with the mass, I should par-
take of the strength of the mass; I should be supported by the mass,
and I should have the same incentives to endeavor with the mass of
my fellow-men; it would be no particular burden, no particular deprivation; but here, where universal suffrage is the rule, where that is the
fundamental idea of the Government, to rule us out is to make us an
exception, to brand us with the stigma of inferiority, and to invite to
our heads the missiles of those about us; therefore, I want the franchise
for the black man. . . .[1]

Reply to President Johnson

Mr. President: In consideration of a delicate sense of propriety as well
as of your repeated intimations of indisposition to discuss or listen to a
reply to the views and opinions you were pleased to express to us in
your elaborate speech today, the undersigned would respectfully take
this method of replying thereto. Believing as we do that the views and
opinions you expressed in that address are entirely unsound and preju-

dicial to the highest interests of our race as well as to our country at large, we cannot do other than expose the same and, as far as may be in our power, arrest their dangerous influence. It is not necessary at this time to call attention to more than two or three features of your remarkable address:

1. The first point to which we feel especially bound to take exception is your attempt to found a policy opposed to our enfranchisement, upon the alleged ground of an existing hostility on the part of the former slaves toward the poor white people of the South. We admit the existence of this hostility, and hold that it is entirely reciprocal. But you obviously commit an error by drawing an argument from an incident of slavery, and making it a basis for a policy adapted to a state of freedom. The hostility between the whites and blacks of the South is easily explained. It has its root and sap in the relation of slavery, and was incited on both sides by the cunning of the slave masters. Those masters secured their ascendency over both the poor whites and blacks by putting enmity between them.

They divided both to conquer each. There was no earthly reason why the blacks should not hate and dread the poor whites when in a state of slavery, for it was from this class that their masters received their slave catchers, slave drivers, and overseers. They were the men called in upon all occasions by the masters whenever any fiendish outrage was to be committed upon the slave. Now, sir, you cannot but perceive, that the cause of this hatred removed, the effect must be removed also. Slavery is abolished. The cause of this antagonism is removed, and you must see that it is altogether illogical (and "putting new wine into old bottles") to legislate from slaveholding and slave-driving premises for a people whom you have repeatedly declared it your purpose to maintain in freedom.

2. Besides, even if it were true, as you allege, that the hostility of the blacks toward the poor whites must necessarily project itself into a state of freedom, and that this enmity between the two races is even more intense in a state of freedom than in a state of slavery, in the name of heaven, we reverently ask how can you, in view of your professed desire to promote the welfare of the black man, deprive him of all means of defence, and clothe him whom you regard as his enemy in the panoply of political power? Can it be that you recommend a policy which would arm the strong and cast down the defenceless? Can you, by any possibility of reasoning, regard this as just, fair, or wise?

Experience proves that those are most abused who can be abused with the greatest impunity. Men are whipped oftenest who are whipped easiest. Peace between races is not to be secured by degrading one race and exalting another; by giving power to one race and withholding it from another; *but* by maintaining a state of equal justice between all classes. First pure, then peaceable.

3. On the colonization theory you were pleased to broach, very much could be said. It is impossible to suppose, in view of the useful-ness of the black man in time of peace as a laborer in the South, and in time of war as a soldier at the North, and the growing respect for his rights among the people and his increasing adaptation to a high state of civilization in his native land, that there can ever come a time when he can be removed from this country without a terrible shock to its prosperity and peace.

Besides, the worst enemy of the nation could not cast upon its fair name a greater infamy than to admit that Negroes could be tolerated among them in a state of the most degrading slavery and oppression, and must be cast away, driven into exile, for no other cause than hav-ing been freed from their chains.[2]

Why Reconstruction Failed

How stands the case with the recently emancipated millions of Negro people in our own country? What is their condition today? What is their relation to the people who formerly held them as slaves? These are important questions, and they are such as trouble the minds of thoughtful men of all colors, at home and abroad. By law, by the Constitution of the United States, slavery has no existence in our country. The legal form has been abolished. By the law and the Constitution, the Negro is a man and a citizen, and has all the rights and liberties guaranteed to any other variety of the human family, residing in the United States.

He has a country, a flag, and a government, and may legally claim full and complete protection under the laws. It was the ruling wish, in-tention, and purpose of the loyal people, after rebellion was suppressed, to have an end to the entire cause of that calamity by forever putting away the system of slavery and all its incidents. In pursuance of this idea, the Negro was made free, made a citizen, made eligible to hold office, to be a juryman, a legislator, and a magistrate. To this end, sev-eral amendments to the Constitution were proposed, recommended, and adopted. They are now a part of the supreme law of the land, bind-ing alike upon every State and Territory of the United States, North and South. Briefly, this is our legal and theoretical condition. This is our condition on paper and parchment. If only from the national statute book we were left to learn the true condition of the Negro race, the result would be altogether creditable to the American people. It would give them a clear title to a place among the most enlightened and liberal nations of the world. We could say of our country, as Curran once said of England, "The spirit of British laws makes liberty commensurate with and inseparable from the British soil." Now I say that this eloquent tribute to England, if only we looked into our Constitution, might apply to us. In that instrument we have laid down the law, now and forever, that there shall be no slavery or involuntary servitude in this republic, except for crime.

We have gone still further. We have laid the heavy hand of the Constitution upon the matchless meanness of caste, as well as upon the hell-black crime of slavery. We have declared before all the world that there shall be no denial of rights on account of race, color, or previous condition of servitude. The advantage gained in this respect is immense.

It is a great thing to have the supreme law of the land on the side of justice and liberty. It is the line up to which the nation is destined to march—the law to which the nation's life must ultimately conform. It is a great principle, up to which we may educate the people, and to this extent its value exceeds all speech.

But today, in most of the Southern States, the Fourteenth and Fifteenth Amendments are virtually nullified.

The rights which they were intended to guarantee are denied and held in contempt. The citizenship granted in the Fourteenth Amendment is practically a mockery, and the right to vote, provided for in the Fifteenth Amendment, is literally stamped out in face of government. The old master class is today triumphant, and the newly enfranchised class in a condition but little above that in which they were found before the rebellion.

Do you ask me how, after all that has been done, this state of things has been made possible? I will tell you. Our Reconstruction measures were radically defective. They left the former slave completely in the power of the old master, the loyal citizen in the hands of the disloyal rebel against the government. Wise, grand, and comprehensive in scope and design as were the Reconstruction measures, high and honorable as were the intentions of the statesmen by whom they were framed and adopted, time and experience, which try all things, have demonstrated that they did not successfully meet the case.

In the hurry and confusion of the hour, and the eager desire to have the Union restored, there was more care for the sublime superstructure of the Republic than for the solid foundation upon which it could alone be upheld. To the freedmen was given the machinery of liberty, but there was denied to them the steam to put it in motion. They were given the uniform of soldiers, but no arms; they were called citizens, but left subjects; they were called free, but left almost slaves. The old master class was not deprived of the power of life and death, which was the soul of the relation of master and slave. They could not, of course, sell their former slaves, but they retained the power to starve them to death, and wherever this power is held there is the power of slavery. He who can say to his fellow-man, "You shall serve me or starve," is a master and his subject is a slave. This was seen and felt by Thaddeus Stevens, Charles Sumner, and leading stalwart Republicans; and had their counsels prevailed the terrible evils from which we now suffer would have been averted. The Negro today would not be on his knees, as he is, abjectly supplicating the old master class to give him leave to toil. Nor would he now be leaving the South as from a doomed city, and seeking a home in the uncongenial North, but tilling his native soil in comparative independence. Though no longer a slave, he is in a thralldom grievous and intolerable, compelled to work for whatever his employer is pleased to pay him, swindled out of his hard earnings by money orders redeemed in stores, compelled to pay the price of an acre of ground for its use during a single year, to pay four times more than a fair price for a pound of bacon and to be kept upon the narrowest margin between life and starvation. Much complaint has been made that the freedmen have shown so little ability to take care of themselves since their Emancipation. Men have marvelled that they have made so little progress. I question the justice of this complaint. It is neither reasonable, nor in any sense just. To me the wonder is, not that the freedmen have made so little progress, but, rather, that they have made so much; not that they have been standing still, but that they have been able to stand at all.

We have only to reflect for a moment upon the situation in which these people found themselves when liberated. Consider their ignorance, their poverty, their destitution, and their absolute dependence upon the very class by which they had been held in bondage for centuries, a class whose very sentiment was averse to their freedom, and we shall be prepared to marvel that they have, under the circumstances, done so well.

History does not furnish an example of Emancipation under conditions less friendly to the emancipated class than this American example. Liberty came to the freedmen of the United States not in mercy, but in wrath, not by moral choice, but by military necessity, not by the generous action of the people among whom they were to live, and whose good-will was essential to the success of the measure, but by strangers, foreigners, invaders, trespassers, aliens, and enemies. The very manner of their Emancipation invited to the heads of the freedmen the bitterest hostility of race and class. They were hated because they had been slaves, hated because they were now free, and hated because of those who had freed them. Nothing was to have been expected other than what has happened, and he is a poor student of the human heart who does not see that the old master class would naturally employ every power and means in their reach to make the great measure of Emancipation unsuccessful and utterly odious. It was born in the tempest and whirlwind of war, and has lived in a storm of violence and blood. When the Hebrews were emancipated, they were told to take spoil from the Egyptians. When the serfs of Russia were emancipated, they were given three acres of ground upon which they could live and make a living. But not so when our slaves were emancipated. . . . They were sent away empty-handed, without money, without friends and without a foot of land upon which to stand. Old and young, sick and well, were turned loose to the open sky, naked to their enemies. The old slave quarter that had before sheltered them and the fields that had yielded them corn were now denied them. The old master class, in its wrath, said, "Clear out! The Yankees have freed you, now let them feed and shelter you!"[3]

Why Has the Negro of the Plantation Made So Little Progress?

Do you ask a more particular answer to the question, why the Negro of the plantation has made so little progress, why his cupboard is empty, why he flutters in rags, why his children run naked, and his wife is barefooted and hides herself behind the hut when a stranger is passing? I will tell you. It is because the husband and father is systematically and almost universally cheated out of his hard earnings. The same class that once extorted his labor under the lash, now extorts his labor by a mean, sneaking, and fraudulent device, which is more effective than the lash. That device is the trucking system, a system which never permits him to see or save a dollar of his hard earnings. He struggles from year to year, but like a man in a morass, the more he struggles, the deeper he sinks. The highest wages paid him are eight dollars a month, and this he receives only in orders on a store, which in many cases is owned by his employer. This scrip has a purchasing power on that one store, and that one store only. A blind man can see that by this arrangement the laborer is bound hand and foot, and he is completely in the power of his employer. He can charge the poor fellow just what he pleases and give what kind of goods he pleases, and he does both. His victim cannot go to another store and buy, and this the storekeeper knows. The only security the wretched Negro has under this arrangement is the conscience of the storekeeper—a conscience educated in the school of slavery, where the idea prevailed in theory and practice that the Negro had no rights which the white men were bound to respect, an arrangement in which everything in the way of food or clothing, whether tainted meat or damaged cloth, is deemed good enough for the Negro. For these he is often made to pay a double price. But this is not all, or the worst result of the system. It puts out of the power of the Negro to save anything of what he earns. If a man gets an honest dollar for his day's work, he has a motive for laying it by and saving it for future emergency. It will be as good for use in the future, and perhaps better a year hence than now; but this miserable scrip has in no sense the quality of a dollar. It is only good at one store and for a limited period. Thus the man who has it is tempted to get rid of it as soon as possible. It may be out of date before he knows it, or the storekeeper may move away and it may be left worthless on his hands. . . .

I ask again, in view of it all, how in the name of human reason could the Negro be expected to make progress, or rise higher in the scale of morals, manners, religion, and civilization than he has done during the twenty years of his so-called freedom? Shame! Eternal shame on those writers and speakers who taunt, denounce, and disparage the Negro, because he is today found in poverty, rags and wretchedness![4]

IV. THE DEMOCRATIC SPIRIT

On Prejudice

THE LESSON of all the ages on this point is, that a wrong done to one man, is a wrong done to all men. It may not be felt at the moment, and the evil day may be long delayed, but so sure as there is a moral government of the universe, so sure will the harvest of evil come.

Color prejudice is not the only prejudice against which a Republic like ours should guard. The spirit of caste is dangerous everywhere. There is the prejudice of the rich against the poor, the pride and prejudice of the idle dandy against the hard handed working man. There is, worst of all, religious prejudice; a prejudice which has stained a whole continent with blood. It is, in fact, a spirit infernal, against which every enlightened man should wage perpetual war.[1]

Woman's Rights

When the true history of the Anti-Slavery cause shall be written, women will occupy a large space in its pages; for the cause of the slave has been peculiarly woman's cause. Her heart and her conscience have supplied in large degree its motive and mainspring. Her skill, industry, patience, and perseverance have been wonderfully manifest in every trial hour. Not only did her feet run on "willing errands," and her fingers do the work which in large degree supplied the sinews of war, but her deep moral convictions, and her tender human sensibilities, found convincing and persuasive expression by her pen and her voice. . . .

Observing woman's agency, devotion, and efficiency in pleading the cause of the slave, gratitude for this high service early moved me to give favorable attention to the subject of what is called "woman's rights" and caused me to be denominated a woman's-rights man. I am glad to say that I have never been ashamed to be thus designated. Recognizing not sex nor physical strength, but moral intelligence and the ability to discern right from wrong, good from evil, and the power to choose between them, as the true basis of republican government, to which all are alike subject and all bound alike to obey, I was not long in reaching the conclusion that there was no foundation in reason or justice for woman's exclusion from the right of choice in the selection of the persons who should frame the laws, and thus shape the destiny of all the people, irrespective of sex.

In a conversation with Mrs. Elizabeth Cady Stanton when she was yet a young lady and an earnest Abolitionist, she was at the pains of setting before me in a very strong light the wrong and injustice of this exclusion. I could not meet her arguments except with the shallow plea of "custom," "natural division of duties," "indelicacy of woman's taking part in politics," the common talk of "woman's sphere," and the like, all of which that able woman, who was then no less logical than now, brushed away by those arguments which she has so often and effectively used since, and which no man has yet successfully refuted.

If intelligence is the only true and rational basis of government, it follows that that is the best government which draws its life and power from the largest sources of wisdom, energy, and goodness at its command. The force of this reasoning would be easily comprehended and readily assented to in any case involving the employment of physical strength. We should all see the folly and madness of attempting to accomplish with a part what could only be done with the united strength of the whole. Though this folly may be less apparent, it is just as real when one-half of the moral and intellectual power of the world is excluded from any voice or vote in civil government.

In this denial of the right to participate in government, not merely the degradation of woman and the perpetuation of a great injustice happens, but the maiming and repudiation of one-half of the moral and intellectual power of the government of the world. Thus far all human governments have been failures, for none have secured, except in a partial degree, the ends for which governments are instituted.

War, slavery, injustice and oppression, and the idea that might makes right have been uppermost in all such governments, and the weak, for whose protection governments are ostensibly created, have had practically no rights which the strong have felt bound to respect. The slayers of thousands have been exalted into heroes, and the worship of mere physical force has been considered glorious. Nations have been and still are but armed camps, expending their wealth and strength and ingenuity in forging weapons of destruction against each other; and while it may not be contended that the introduction of the feminine element in government would entirely cure this tendency to exalt might over right, many reasons can be given to show that woman's influence would greatly tend to check and modify this barbarous and destructive tendency.

At any rate, seeing that the male governments of the world have failed, it can do no harm to try the experiment of a government by man and woman united. But it is not my purpose to argue the question here, but simply to state in a brief way the ground of my espousal of the cause of woman's suffrage. I believed that the exclusion of my race from participation in government was not only wrong, but a great mistake, because it took from that race motives for high thought and endeavor and degraded them in the eyes of the world around them. Man derives a sense of his consequence in the world not merely subjectively, but objectively. If from the cradle through life the outside world brands a class as unfit for this or that work, the character of the class will come to resemble and conform to the character described. To find valuable qualities in our fellows, such qualities must be presumed and expected.

I would give woman a vote, give her a motive to qualify herself to vote, precisely as I insisted upon giving the colored man the right to vote; in order that she shall have the same motives for making herself a useful citizen as those in force in the case of other citizens. In a word, I have never yet been able to find one consideration, one argument, or suggestion in favor of man's right to participate in civil government which did not equally apply to the right of woman.[2]

When a great truth once gets abroad in the world, no power on earth can imprison it, or prescribe its limits, or suppress it. It is bound to go on till it becomes the thought of the world. Such a truth is woman's right to equal liberty with man. She was born with it. It was hers before she comprehended it. It is prescribed upon all the powers and faculties of her soul, and no custom, law nor usage can ever destroy it. Now that it has got fairly fixed in the minds of the few, it is bound to become fixed in the minds of the many, and be supported at last by a great cloud of witnesses, which no man can number and no power can withstand.[3]

The Elevation of Labor

Our sympathies, as far as the diminution of work is concerned, are naturally enlisted on the side of the laborers. . . . It is incontrovertible and evident that ten hours' uninterrupted hard work, with the addition of the time required to go to the factory and back, will, in the long run, reduce the laborer to the level of a beast of burden. . . . The uniform, mechanical, and exhausting factory work, which keeps him busy uninterruptedly year after year, without offering him any prospect of ever becoming independent, nay, of ever achieving more than keeps starvation from his door, cannot fail either to make him desperate, or to smother all higher impulses and aspirations in him. If he has a desire to improve and instruct himself, he cannot gratify it, because, unless endowed with uncommon physical and mental powers, he will be too worn-out after having got through his daily task to devote the few remaining hours to anything but absolute rest. The natural right of man to a certain extent of recreation and enjoyment is disregarded in his case, and thus generation after generation has dragged along an existence full of hardship and privation, in hopeless poverty. Indeed, the old system of factory labor is but another remnant of the bad old times when the laborer himself was considered hardly worth as much as the machine he worked; a thing to be used to its utmost capacity, not fit for instruction and improvement. Those abuses we are outgrowing, however, and not even the conservatism of monarchial Europe can stem the tide of modern ideas, to whose leveling influence all, the high as well as the low, will have to submit in the course of time.[4]

An Industrial College

What can be done to improve the condition of the free colored people in the United States? The plan which I humbly submit in answer to this inquiry . . . is the establishment . . . of an INDUSTRIAL COLLEGE, in which shall be taught several important branches of the mechanical arts. This college to be open to colored youth. . . . The fact is (every day begins with the lesson, and ends with the lesson) that colored men must learn trades—must find new employments, new modes of usefulness to society—or that they must decay under the pressing wants to which their condition is rapidly bringing them. We must become mechanics—we must build, as well as live in houses—we must make, as well as use furniture—we must construct bridges, as well as pass over them—before we can properly live, or be respected by our fellow men. We need mechanics, as well as ministers. We need workers in iron, wood, clay, and in leather. We have orators, authors, and other professional men; but these reach only a certain class, and get respect for our race in certain select circles. To live here as we ought, we must fasten ourselves to our countrymen through their every day and cardinal wants. We must not only be able to *black* boots, but to *make* them. At present, we are unknown in the Northern States, as mechanics. We give no proof of genius or skill at the County, the State, or the National Fairs. We are unknown at any of the great exhibitions of the industry of our fellow-citizens—and being unknown, we are unconsidered.

The fact that we make no show of our ability, is held conclusive of our inability to make any. Hence, all the indifference and contempt, with which incapacity is regarded, fall upon us, and that too, when we have had no means of disproving the injurious opinion of our natural inferiority. I have, during the last dozen years, denied, before the Americans, that we are an inferior race. But this has been done by arguments, based upon admitted principles, rather than by the presentation of facts. Now, firmly believing, as I do, that there are skill, invention, power, industry, and real mechanical genius among the colored people, which will bear favorable testimony for them, and which only need the means to develop them, I am decidedly in favor of the establishment of such a college as I have mentioned. The benefits of such an institution would not be confined to the Northern States, nor to the free colored people: they would extend over the whole Union. The slave, not less than the freeman, would be benefitted by such an institution. It must be confessed that the most powerful argument, now used by the Southern slave-holder—and the one most soothing to his conscience—is, that derived from the low condition of the free colored people at the North. I have long felt that too little attention has been given, by our truest friends, in this country, to removing this stumbling block out of the way of the slave's liberation.

The most telling, the most killing refutation of slavery, is the presentation of an industrious, enterprising, upright, thrifty and intelligent free black population. Such a population, I believe, would rise in the Northern States, under the fostering care of such a College as that supposed.

To show that we are capable of becoming mechanics, I might adduce any amount of testimony; but dear Madam, I need not ring the changes on such a proposition. There is no question in the mind of any unprejudiced person, that the Negro is capable of making a good mechanic. Indeed, even those who cherish the bitterest feelings towards us have admitted that the apprehension that Negroes might be employed in their stead, dictated the policy of excluding them from trades altogether; but I will not dwell upon this point, as I fear I have already trespassed too long upon your precious time, and written more than I ought to expect you to read. Allow me to say, in conclusion, that I believe every intelligent colored man in America will approve and rejoice at the establishment of some such institution as that now suggested. There are many respectable colored men, fathers of large families, having boys nearly grown up, whose minds are tossed by day and by night, with the anxious enquiry, what shall I do with my boys? Such an institution would meet the wants of such persons.[5]

REFERENCE NOTES

A TRIBUNE OF HIS PEOPLE

1. Douglass to Mrs. Livermore, Apr. 4, 1885, Douglass *mss.*, Frederick Douglass Memorial Home, Anacostia, D. C.

2. Philip S. Foner, *Business and Slavery* (Chapel Hill, 1941), p. 1.

3. See Dorothy B. Porter, "David B. Ruggles, an Apostle of Human Freedom," *Journal of Negro History*, 1943, Vol. XXVIII, pp. 23–50.

4. Jane Marsh Parker, "Reminiscences of Frederick Douglass," *The Outlook*, Apr. 6, 1895, p. 553.

5. *Liberator*, Oct. 29, 1841.

6. *Tenth Annual Report of the Board of Managers of the Massachusetts Anti-Slavery Society*, 1842, pp. 105–06.

7. *Liberator*, Jan. 29, 1846.

8. *Ibid.*, Mar. 27, 1846.

9. *Ibid.*, June 8, 1849.

10. *London Times*, Apr. 6, 1847.

11. *Farewell Speech of Mr. Frederick Douglass at the London Tavern*, London, 1847, p. 21.

12. *Liberator*, June 8, 1849.

13. Charles H. Wesley, "The Negroes of New York in the Emancipation Movement," *Journal of Negro History*, Vol. XXIV, Jan., 1939, p. 98.

14. Douglass to Gerrit Smith, Mar. 30, 1849, Smith *mss.*, Syracuse University Library.

15. *New York Tribune*, Sept. 18, 1857.

16. Douglass to Gerrit Smith, Mar. 30, 1849, Smith *mss.*, Syracuse University Library.

17. Benjamin Quarles, "Frederick Douglass and Woman's Rights," *Journal of Negro History*, Vol. XXV, Jan., 1940, pp. 35, 44.

18. *The Woman's Journal*, Apr. 14, 1888.

19. *Frederick Douglass' Paper*, May 19, 1854. *See also* Horace McGuire, "Two Episodes of Anti-Slavery Days," *Publications of the Rochester Historical Society*, 1925, Vol. IV, p. 209.

20. Sarah H. Bradford, *Scenes in the Life of Harriet Tubman* (Auburn, New York, 1869), p. 233. *See also* Earl Conrad, *Harriet Tubman* (New York, 1942).

21. Oliver Johnson, *William Lloyd*

Garrison and His Times (Boston, 1880), p. 314.

22. *Liberator*, Nov. 26, 1841. *See also* Herbert Aptheker, "Militant Abolitionism," *Journal of Negro History*, Vol. XXVI, Oct., 1941, pp. 413–84; *also* Herbert Aptheker, *The Negro in the Abolitionist Movement* (New York, 1941).

23. *Liberator*, June 8, 1849.

24. *New York Herald*, Aug. 12, 1852.

25. *Frederick Douglass' Paper*, Nov. 28, 1856. *See also* William Chambers, *American Slavery and Colour* (New York, 1857), p. 174.

26. *The North Star*, reprinted in the *Liberator*, May 23, 1851. *See also* Benjamin Quarles, "The Breach between Douglass and Garrison," *Journal of Negro History*, Vol. XXIII, Apr., 1938, p. 150. Douglass' letters to Gerrit Smith deal with this question in detail.

27. See Douglass' lectures, *The Anti-Slavery Movement* (Rochester, 1855), and *The Constitution of the United States: Is It Pro-Slavery or Anti-Slavery* (Scotland, 1860).

28. *Frederick Douglass' Paper*, Apr. 25, 1856; *Liberator*, Sept. 5, 1856.

29. *Frederick Douglass' Paper*, Apr. 25, 1856; *Liberator*, Sept. 5, 1856; Douglass to Gerrit Smith, Apr. 30, 1857, Smith *mss.*, Syracuse University Library.

30. *Life and Times of Frederick Douglass*, p. 390; Oswald Garrison Villard, *John Brown* (New York, 1943), pp. 320–23.

31. Villard, *op. cit.*, pp. 323, 627. *See also* Leonard Ehrlich, *God's Angry Man* (New York, 1932).

32. See Douglass' letter in Elizabeth Keckley, *Behind the Scenes or Thirty Years a Slave and Four Years in the White House* (New York, 1868), p. 319.

33. *John Brown, an address by Frederick Douglass at the Fourteenth Anniversary of Storer College, Harper's Ferry, West Va., May 30, 1881*, pp. 12–14.

34. *Proceedings of the Colored National Convention held in Rochester, July 6th, 7th and 8th, 1853*, p. 19.

35. *Douglass' Monthly*, Feb., Mar., 1861.

36. *Ibid.*, Feb., 1863.

37. Allen Thorndike Rice, ed., *Reminiscences of Abraham Lincoln by Distinguished Men of his Time* (New York, 1886), pp. 185–88.

38. *Proceedings of the Thirteenth Anniversary meeting of the American Anti-Slavery Society*, 1864, p. 118.

39. *New York Tribune*, Jan. 30, Mar. 12, 1866; *Atlantic Monthly*, Dec., 1866, p. 762.

40. Edward McPherson, *The Political History of the United States During the Period of Reconstruction*, (Washington, 1880), pp. 52–55.

41. Frederick May Holland,

Frederick Douglass (New York, 1891), pp. 317–18.

42. *New York Herald*, Sept. 7, 1866.

43. Douglass to Elizabeth Cady Stanton, Feb. 6, 1882, Douglass *mss.*, Frederick Douglass Memorial Home, Anacostia, D. C.

44. *Emancipation Address by Frederick Douglass* (Washington, 1888), p. 8.

45. *New National Era*, May 26, 1870.

46. *Speech of Frederick Douglass at the Civil Rights Mass Meeting at Lincoln Hall, October 22, 1883* (Washington, D. C., 1883), p. 8.

47. Douglass to W. J. Wilson, Aug. 8, 1865, Douglass *mss.*, Frederick Douglass Memorial Home, Anacostia, D. C.

SLAVERY

1. From reception speech at Finsbury Chapel, Moorefield, England, May 12, 1846.

2. From speech at Rochester, July 5, 1852.

3. *Ibid.*

4. From *Life and Times of Frederick Douglass*, pp. 180–81.

5. From speech at Rochester, Dec. 1, 1850.

6. From speech at Rochester, July 5, 1852.

7. From speech in Faneuil Hall, Boston, June 8, 1849.

8. From letter to Mrs. Harriet Beecher Stowe, Rochester, Mar. 8, 1853.

9. From letter to Samuel Hanson Cox, D.D., Edinburgh, Oct. 30, 1846.

10. From reception speech at Finsbury Chapel, Moorefield, England, May 12, 1846.

11. From speech at Glasgow, Scotland, May 29, 1846.

12. From lecture, *The Anti-Slavery Movement*, Rochester, 1885.

13. From lecture, *The Slavery Party*, May, 1855.

14. From address on West India Emancipation, Aug. 4, 1857.

THE CIVIL WAR

1. From editorial in *Douglass' Monthly*, May, 1861.

2. From *Life and Times of Frederick Douglass*, pp. 340–42.

3. *Ibid.*, pp. 344–46.

4. From speech at National Hall, Philadelphia, July 6, 1863.

5. From Allen Thorndike Rice, ed., *Reminiscences of Abraham Lincoln*, pp. 185–88.

6. From Decoration Day address at Arlington, 1882.

RECONSTRUCTION

1. From speech at the annual meeting of the Massachusetts Anti-Slavery Society, Boston, 1865.

2. From *Life and Times of Frederick Douglass*, pp. 391–92.

3. From West India Emancipation Speech, Elmira, N. Y., Aug. 1, 1880.

4. From Emancipation Address. Washington, 1888.

THE DEMOCRATIC SPIRIT

1. From speech at Civil Rights Mass Meeting, October 22, 1883.

2. From *Life and Times of Frederick Douglass*, pp. 473–82.

3. From speech before the International Council of Women, Washington, D. C., Mar. 31, 1888.

4. From *The New National Era*, Oct. 26, 1871.

5. From letter to Harriet Beecher Stowe, Mar. 8, 1853, in *Life and Times of Frederick Douglass*, pp. 291–95.

DOVER·THRIFT·EDITIONS

FICTION

A JOURNAL OF THE PLAGUE YEAR, Daniel Defoe. 192pp. 41919-3
SIX GREAT SHERLOCK HOLMES STORIES, Sir Arthur Conan Doyle. 112pp. 27055-6
SHORT STORIES, Theodore Dreiser. 112pp. 28215-5
SILAS MARNER, George Eliot. 160pp. 29246-0
JOSEPH ANDREWS, Henry Fielding. 288pp. 41588-0
THIS SIDE OF PARADISE, F. Scott Fitzgerald. 208pp. 28999-0
"THE DIAMOND AS BIG AS THE RITZ" AND OTHER STORIES, F. Scott Fitzgerald. 29991-0
MADAME BOVARY, Gustave Flaubert. 256pp. 29257-6
THE REVOLT OF "MOTHER" AND OTHER STORIES, Mary E. Wilkins Freeman. 128pp.
  40428-5
A ROOM WITH A VIEW, E. M. Forster. 176pp. (Available in U.S. only.) 28467-0
WHERE ANGELS FEAR TO TREAD, E. M. Forster. 128pp. (Available in U.S. only.) 27791-7
THE IMMORALIST, André Gide. 112pp. (Available in U.S. only.) 29237-1
HERLAND, Charlotte Perkins Gilman. 128pp. 40429-3
"THE YELLOW WALLPAPER" AND OTHER STORIES, Charlotte Perkins Gilman. 80pp. 29857-4
THE OVERCOAT AND OTHER STORIES, Nikolai Gogol. 112pp. 27057-2
CHELKASH AND OTHER STORIES, Maxim Gorky. 64pp. 40652-0
GREAT GHOST STORIES, John Grafton (ed.). 112pp. 27270-2
DETECTION BY GASLIGHT, Douglas G. Greene (ed.). 272pp. 29928-7
THE MABINOGION, Lady Charlotte E. Guest. 192pp. 29541-9
"THE FIDDLER OF THE REELS" AND OTHER SHORT STORIES, Thomas Hardy. 80pp. 29960-0
THE LUCK OF ROARING CAMP AND OTHER STORIES, Bret Harte. 96pp. 27271-0
THE HOUSE OF THE SEVEN GABLES, Nathaniel Hawthorne. 272pp. 40882-5
THE SCARLET LETTER, Nathaniel Hawthorne. 192pp. 28048-9
YOUNG GOODMAN BROWN AND OTHER STORIES, Nathaniel Hawthorne. 128pp. 27060-2
THE GIFT OF THE MAGI AND OTHER SHORT STORIES, O. Henry. 96pp. 27061-0
THE NUTCRACKER AND THE GOLDEN POT, E. T. A. Hoffmann. 128pp. 27806-9
THE ASPERN PAPERS, Henry James. 112pp. 41922-3
THE BEAST IN THE JUNGLE AND OTHER STORIES, Henry James. 128pp. 27552-3
DAISY MILLER, Henry James. 64pp. 28773-4
THE TURN OF THE SCREW, Henry James. 96pp. 26684-2
WASHINGTON SQUARE, Henry James. 176pp. 40431-5
THE COUNTRY OF THE POINTED FIRS, Sarah Orne Jewett. 96pp. 28196-5
THE AUTOBIOGRAPHY OF AN EX-COLORED MAN, James Weldon Johnson. 112pp. 28512-X
DUBLINERS, James Joyce. 160pp. 26870-5
A PORTRAIT OF THE ARTIST AS A YOUNG MAN, James Joyce. 192pp. 28050-0
THE METAMORPHOSIS AND OTHER STORIES, Franz Kafka. 96pp. 29030-1
THE MAN WHO WOULD BE KING AND OTHER STORIES, Rudyard Kipling. 128pp. 28051-9
YOU KNOW ME AL, Ring Lardner. 128pp. 28513-8
SELECTED SHORT STORIES, D. H. Lawrence. 128pp. 27794-1
GREEN TEA AND OTHER GHOST STORIES, J. Sheridan LeFanu. 96pp. 27795-X
THE CALL OF THE WILD, Jack London. 64pp. 26472-6
FIVE GREAT SHORT STORIES, Jack London. 96pp. 27063-7
THE SEA-WOLF, Jack London. 248pp. 41108-7
WHITE FANG, Jack London. 160pp. 26968-X
DEATH IN VENICE, Thomas Mann. 96pp. (Available in U.S. only.) 28714-9
IN A GERMAN PENSION: 13 Stories, Katherine Mansfield. 112pp. 28719-X
THE NECKLACE AND OTHER SHORT STORIES, Guy de Maupassant. 128pp. 27064-5
BARTLEBY AND BENITO CERENO, Herman Melville. 112pp. 26473-4
THE OIL JAR AND OTHER STORIES, Luigi Pirandello. 96pp. 28459-X
THE GOLD-BUG AND OTHER TALES, Edgar Allan Poe. 128pp. 26875-6
TALES OF TERROR AND DETECTION, Edgar Allan Poe. 96pp. 28744-0

DOVER · THRIFT · EDITIONS

FICTION

THE QUEEN OF SPADES AND OTHER STORIES, Alexander Pushkin. 128pp. 28054-3

THE STORY OF AN AFRICAN FARM, Olive Schreiner. 256pp. 40165-0

FRANKENSTEIN, Mary Shelley. 176pp. 28211-2

THE JUNGLE, Upton Sinclair. 320pp. (Available in U.S. only.) 41923-1

THREE LIVES, Gertrude Stein. 176pp. (Available in U.S. only.) 28059-4

THE BODY SNATCHER AND OTHER TALES, Robert Louis Stevenson. 80pp. 41924-X

THE STRANGE CASE OF DR. JEKYLL AND MR. HYDE, Robert Louis Stevenson. 64pp. 26688-5

TREASURE ISLAND, Robert Louis Stevenson. 160pp. 27559-0

GULLIVER'S TRAVELS, Jonathan Swift. 240pp. 29273-8

THE KREUTZER SONATA AND OTHER SHORT STORIES, Leo Tolstoy. 144pp. 27805-0

THE WARDEN, Anthony Trollope. 176pp. 40076-X

FIRST LOVE AND DIARY OF A SUPERFLUOUS MAN, Ivan Turgenev. 96pp. 28775-0

FATHERS AND SONS, Ivan Turgenev. 176pp. 40073-5

ADVENTURES OF HUCKLEBERRY FINN, Mark Twain. 224pp. 28061-6

THE ADVENTURES OF TOM SAWYER, Mark Twain. 192pp. 40077-8

THE MYSTERIOUS STRANGER AND OTHER STORIES, Mark Twain. 128pp. 27069-6

HUMOROUS STORIES AND SKETCHES, Mark Twain. 80pp. 29279-7

AROUND THE WORLD IN EIGHTY DAYS, Jules Verne. 160pp. 41111-7

CANDIDE, Voltaire (François-Marie Arouet). 112pp. 26689-3

GREAT SHORT STORIES BY AMERICAN WOMEN, Candace Ward (ed.). 192pp. 28776-9

"THE COUNTRY OF THE BLIND" AND OTHER SCIENCE-FICTION STORIES, H. G. Wells. 160pp. (Not available in Europe or United Kingdom.) 29569-9

THE ISLAND OF DR. MOREAU, H. G. Wells. 112pp. (Not available in Europe or United Kingdom.) 29027-1

THE INVISIBLE MAN, H. G. Wells. 112pp. (Not available in Europe or United Kingdom.) 27071-8

THE TIME MACHINE, H. G. Wells. 80pp. (Not available in Europe or United Kingdom.) 28472-7

THE WAR OF THE WORLDS, H. G. Wells. 160pp. (Not available in Europe or United Kingdom.) 29506-0

ETHAN FROME, Edith Wharton. 96pp. 26690-7

SHORT STORIES, Edith Wharton. 128pp. 28235-X

THE AGE OF INNOCENCE, Edith Wharton. 288pp. 29803-5

THE PICTURE OF DORIAN GRAY, Oscar Wilde. 192pp. 27807-7

JACOB'S ROOM, Virginia Woolf. 144pp. (Not available in Europe or United Kingdom.) 40109-X

MONDAY OR TUESDAY: Eight Stories, Virginia Woolf. 64pp. (Not available in Europe or United Kingdom.) 29453-6

NONFICTION

POETICS, Aristotle. 64pp. 29577-X

POLITICS, Aristotle. 368pp. 41424-8

NICOMACHEAN ETHICS, Aristotle. 256pp. 40096-4

MEDITATIONS, Marcus Aurelius. 128pp. 29823-X

THE LAND OF LITTLE RAIN, Mary Austin. 96pp. 29037-9

THE DEVIL'S DICTIONARY, Ambrose Bierce. 144pp. 27542-6

THE ANALECTS, Confucius. 128pp. 28484-0

CONFESSIONS OF AN ENGLISH OPIUM EATER, Thomas De Quincey. 80pp. 28742-4

THE SOULS OF BLACK FOLK, W. E. B. Du Bois. 176pp. 28041-1

DOVER · THRIFT · EDITIONS

NONFICTION

NARRATIVE OF THE LIFE OF FREDERICK DOUGLASS, Frederick Douglass. 96pp. 28499-9

SELF-RELIANCE AND OTHER ESSAYS, Ralph Waldo Emerson. 128pp. 27790-9

THE LIFE OF OLAUDAH EQUIANO, OR GUSTAVUS VASSA, THE AFRICAN, Olaudah Equiano. 192pp. 40661-X

THE AUTOBIOGRAPHY OF BENJAMIN FRANKLIN, Benjamin Franklin. 144pp. 29073-5

TOTEM AND TABOO, Sigmund Freud. 176pp. (Not available in Europe or United Kingdom.) 40434-X

LOVE: A Book of Quotations, Herb Galewitz (ed.). 64pp. 40004-2

PRAGMATISM, William James. 128pp. 28270-8

THE STORY OF MY LIFE, Helen Keller. 80pp. 29249-5

TAO TE CHING, Lao Tze. 112pp. 29792-6

GREAT SPEECHES, Abraham Lincoln. 112pp. 26872-1

THE PRINCE, Niccolò Machiavelli. 80pp. 27274-5

THE SUBJECTION OF WOMEN, John Stuart Mill. 112pp. 29601-6

SELECTED ESSAYS, Michel de Montaigne. 96pp. 29109-X

UTOPIA, Sir Thomas More. 96pp. 29583-4

BEYOND GOOD AND EVIL: Prelude to a Philosophy of the Future, Friedrich Nietzsche. 176pp. 29868-X

THE BIRTH OF TRAGEDY, Friedrich Nietzsche. 96pp. 28515-4

COMMON SENSE, Thomas Paine. 64pp. 29602-4

SYMPOSIUM AND PHAEDRUS, Plato. 96pp. 27798-4

THE TRIAL AND DEATH OF SOCRATES: Four Dialogues, Plato. 128pp. 27066-1

A MODEST PROPOSAL AND OTHER SATIRICAL WORKS, Jonathan Swift. 64pp. 28759-9

CIVIL DISOBEDIENCE AND OTHER ESSAYS, Henry David Thoreau. 96pp. 27563-9

SELECTIONS FROM THE JOURNALS (Edited by Walter Harding), Henry David Thoreau. 96pp. 28760-2

WALDEN; OR, LIFE IN THE WOODS, Henry David Thoreau. 224pp. 28495-6

NARRATIVE OF SOJOURNER TRUTH, Sojourner Truth. 80pp. 29899-X

THE THEORY OF THE LEISURE CLASS, Thorstein Veblen. 256pp. 28062-4

DE PROFUNDIS, Oscar Wilde. 64pp. 29308-4

OSCAR WILDE'S WIT AND WISDOM: A Book of Quotations, Oscar Wilde. 64pp. 40146-4

UP FROM SLAVERY, Booker T. Washington. 160pp. 28738-6

A VINDICATION OF THE RIGHTS OF WOMAN, Mary Wollstonecraft. 224pp. 29036-0